More Praise for *Coming of Age*

"I loved Anderson, Hill, and Martinson's daring journey into the lives of younger men that we have failed to recognize, appreciate, and minister to. *Coming of Age* extends a hand to this select group and beyond to all who hunger for deeper connections and new meaning as the Body of Christ. *Coming of Age* takes a hard look at the church's shortcomings with these men, offers fresh ideas and challenges for change, and above all reveals the vibrant ministry that these young men could offer back to their communities and the world."
  —*Peter Mayer, singer, songwriter, guitarist of the Peter Mayer Group, and Jimmy Buffett's Coral Reefers*

"Thank you for the opportunity to preview. I have read *Coming of Age* several times and have found it to be the most important book on men's ministries that I have read in many years. The authors show a real concern for the lost tribe of young men in the Christian community.

"As the Christian church has become feminized, many young men have felt lost in the shuffle and returned to the time-honored resources of sports, nature, family, friends, work, and service, to nurture them on their spiritual journey. They seek life-changing experiences to empower them to deal with stress, crisis, and conflict. They depend on the wisdom of older men to guide them in becoming the best men possible. Sadly, the church has not looked at itself to see what has been happening.

"The authors move beyond asking, "Where have all the young men gone?" to suggesting non-traditional ways that congregations might address the development of ministries for young men. With compassion, solid theological understanding, and great creativity, *Coming of Age* provides a guide for denominational leaders, pastors, Christian educators, and education committees to renew men's ministries, and transform the church as we know it.

"To say that this book is important is an understatement. It is a challenge to the Christian community for change, renewal, and an increased commitment to be a transforming community where a new partnership is developed, where a new equality between men and women is practiced, and where people are accepted where they are, as they are, and equipped for life in the real world. This book is a winner!"
  —*Dr. Curtis A. Miller, Past President of the North American Conference of Church Men's Staff, Former Associate of Men's Ministries, Presbyterian Church (USA)*

"Authors Anderson, Hill, and Martinson have heard the voices of young men whose stories reveal depth of spirituality and the workings of faith. In our "feminized churches," these are the marginalized. This is not a critique of women's places in our ministries. It is a corrective to make room for those outside. Truth in love. Buy this book. Read this book. Pray through this book and for women and men to find their place in our churches again."

> —*Pastor Michael Foss, Senior Pastor of Prince of Peace in Burnsville, Minnesota, author of* Power Surge, Real Faith for Real Life, *and* A Servant's Manual

"For years leaders of men's ministries have struggled to find effective avenues to reach young men. We now have a captivating and credible look into their worlds thanks to the research and analysis done by David Anderson, Paul Hill, and Roland Martinson. *Coming of Age* is clear, concise, and captivating. It holds the church both culpable for the absence of these men and capable of meeting the challenge. It gives church leaders seeking to do ministry with men insightful, analytical, and programmatic handles to grasp for launching bold, innovative, and effective ministries with young men. The real question now is whether or not we church leaders have the courage to take firm hold of the handles *Coming of Age* provides us.

> —*J. Gregory Alexander, Acting General Minister, Christian Church (Disciples of Christ) in Kentucky, Lead Author,* The Fellowship of Carpenters, *A Men's Study Series, President, North American Conference of Church Men Staffs*

"*Coming of Age* provides reflective research identifying common themes based on the interviews of eighty-eight young men from very different walks of life and suggestions as to how we can provide opportunities for young men to see God at work in the world and in the church. Young men live in a culture that emphasizes self, work, sports, consumerism, and personal experience. This book suggests how the church can lift up forgiveness, repentance, sacraments, and Holy Scripture. I recommend reading this book to pastors and lay leaders who wish to reach out the young men who are dropping away from the church in record numbers."

> —*Leonard H. Bolick, Bishop, North Carolina Synod, ELCA*

COMING
OF AGE

Exploring the Identity
and Spirituality of Younger Men

David W.   Paul G.   Roland D.
Anderson   Hill   Martinson

Augsburg Fortress
MINNEAPOLIS

COMING OF AGE
Exploring the Identity and Spirituality of Younger Men

Large-quantity purchases or custom editions of this book are available at a discount from the publisher. For more information, contact the sales department at Augsburg Fortress, Publishers, 1-800-328-4648, or write to: Sales Director, Augsburg Fortress, Publishers, P. O. Box 1209, Minneapolis, MN 55440-1209.

Scripture passages are from the New Revised Standard Version of the Bible, copyright © 1946, 1952, 1971, 1989 by the Division of Christian Education of the National Council of the Churches of Christ in the USA. Used by permission.

Page 92: "Loose In The World." Written by Peter Mayer and Jim Mayer. © 2002 Little Flock Music (BMI) / Cliffhanging Music (BMI) / Administered by Bug. All Rights Reserved. Used by permission.

Page 100: "Youth of the Nation", POD, *Satellite,* © 2001 Souljah Music, admin. Famous Music Corp. / Famous Music Corporation. Used by permission.

Page 104: "Father of Mine," Everclear, *So Much for the Afterglow,* © 1997 evergleam music/montalupis music/commongreen music/irving music. All rights reserved. Used by permission.

Library of Congress Cataloging-in-Publication Data
Anderson, David W., 1951-
   Coming of age : exploring the identity and spirituality of younger men / David Anderson, Paul Hill, Roland Martinson.
      p. cm.
   Includes bibliographical references.
   ISBN 0-8066-5224-1 (pbk. : alk. paper)
   1. Young men—Religious life. I. Hill, Paul, Rev. II. Martinson, Roland D., 1942- III. Title.
   BV4541.3.A53 2006
   277.3'08308421—dc22   2005032513

Cover design by Diana Running; Cover photo: © Royalty-Free/Corbis. Used by permission. Book design by Michelle L. N. Cook

The paper used in this publication meets the minimum requirements of American National Standard for Information Sciences—Permanence of Paper for Printed Library Materials, ANSI Z329.48-1984. ⊖ ™

Manufactured in the U.S.A.

10   09   08   07   06   1   2   3   4   5   6   7   8   9   10

CONTENTS

127233

chapter 1

EXPLORING THE IDENTITY AND SPIRITUALITY OF YOUNGER MEN

Where Have All the Young Men Gone?

"Where have all the young men gone?" is a poignant line from a folk song that aptly expresses church leaders' wonderment regarding twenty-first century young adult males' church participation. "Twenty-something" guys are scarce in worship services and acts of ministry these days. More than baffled, parents join pastors and lay leaders in lamenting the disinterest of young men in organized religion.

"Where have all the young men gone?" Why are they gone? What is going on with them and God? Has the church failed to respond to the realities of young men? If one could discover what is going on in their spiritual lives, might such a discovery make a difference to them or to the church? Discovering accurate information about and perhaps even direct answers to these important questions will make a difference in the lives of young men and the church and her ministry.

Most research on "twenty-somethings" and "thirty-some-things" (persons born between 1965 and 1985) doesn't separate data on religious interest by gender. Much of the research indicates that both men and women in this age group are not regularly present in worship or engaging in congregational ministry activities. Of this generation as a whole, 43 percent say they go to church once per month with 32 percent saying they go to church once a year or never.[1]

Nevertheless, the vast majority of this generation consider themselves to be persons of faith: 79 percent say they believe in God; 10 percent see themselves as seekers; 6 percent as agnostic; and 5 percent as atheist.[2]

This young adult post-modern generation seems to possess a skepticism regarding the institutional church, opting rather for making more personal connection with God. In his book, *Postmoderns,* Craig Miller writes, "For post-moderns, belief and attendance at religious services do not necessarily equate. Many feel quite comfortable with the concept that they can maintain their faith without being involved in a faith community. In a survey of twenty-somethings, 60 percent say they do not see the church as the best place to pursue their faith."[3]

The little existing research on the religiosity of young men indicates significantly lesser levels of participation than among young women and that this has been true for at least three generations. According to Gail Malmgreen, in modern western cultures, religion is a predominately female sphere. In nearly every sect and denomination of Christianity, although men monopolize the positions of authority, women participate in greater numbers than men.[4] Michael Argyle writes, "Women are more religious than men on all criteria, particularly for private prayer, also for membership attendance and attitude."[5] "Women are twice as likely to attend a church service during any given week. Women are also 50 percent more likely than men to say they are 'religious' and to state that they are 'absolutely committed' to the Christian faith," according to George Barna.[6]

An experienced college chaplain observes that 70-80 percent of the students involved in campus ministry activities are female, and that he has a hard time persuading young men to get involved.[7] Outdoor ministry directors have long had a difficult time recruiting sufficient numbers of young adult male staff, regularly having to get along with significantly fewer male counselors than they need.

The data and anecdotal experiences do not necessarily indicate that young men are not spiritual, rather it seems that the church in its present expressions of ministry has failed to engage young men's attention and commitment.

If these anecdotal observations and related research findings are reflective of the religious lives of young men, this information raises as many questions and issues as it provides answers. Are young men, in fact, much less involved in church-oriented religious practices as young women? If so, why? What is it about those religious practices that fail to engage them? In spite of their lack of interest in religion, are young men deeply spiritual as some researchers assert? If so, what does their spirituality look like? If one can get at what is true in regard to their faith life, what message might young men have for the church and her ministry?

The Young Male Spirituality Project

With these questions in mind, the Young Male Spirituality Project, a joint effort of Lutheran Men in Mission (LMM) of the Evangelical Lutheran Church in America (ELCA) and Luther Seminary (St. Paul, Minnesota) Faith Factors Research Teams, decided to interview a sample of young men across the United States and hear what they had to say.

Our goal was relatively simple: Identify a variety of young men between the ages of eighteen and thirty-five and listen carefully to what they had to say about their lives, their faith, and their faith practices. Eighty-eight young men of differing faith experiences and four ethnic groups from six regions of the country were contacted and interviewed. These European, African-, Asian-, and Hispanic-American young men also exhibited four expressions of faith in their lives:

1. those who had never been members of a faith tradition;
2. those who had been introduced to a faith community as children, but left at some point on their way to adulthood;
3. those who had come to faith and membership in a church as young adults;
4. those who had been members and actively involved in congregation their entire lives.

This qualitative study, while representative of a wide variety of young men in the United States, is not a quantitative study of a random sample that would be representative of all young men between the ages of eighteen and thirty-five.

Each one hour interview followed a young man's life story into his spirituality or faith with its particular practices. The terms, *spirituality* and *faith* were loosely employed to allow the young man and the interviewer to follow the unique faith experience of each person. Consequently, every interview had its own character as each young man shared from his experience what was most central to his life core, purpose, and relationship with God. The conversations were lively, engaging, even spiritually moving, and transformative. The interviews clearly touched a vital nerve in these young men's lives.

The interviews were analyzed by the three authors of this study who shared their findings with each other. Common themes quickly emerged from the young men's stories and in the analyses of the evaluators. Evaluator differences were checked against the data, and a common report on the findings of the eighty-eight interviews was presented to a representative gathering of sixteen of the young men interviewed. These young men verified that the fullness and authenticity of their experience was accurately represented in the report. The report was well received by the sixteen young men who moved onto further exploration of each other's lives and faith. They began to wonder with each other about the implications of these findings for developing new expressions of faith and ministry.

Young Men's Common Voices—A Message for the Church

The coming of age reflected in the stories of these young men's lives, their excitement in "finding others like them with common faith journeys," and their "message" for the church forms the spirit and purpose of this book. These young men are spiritually complex. Their voices are poignant and powerful. They are multiply spiritually gifted! They present a huge asset as well as a daunting challenge to the church and its ministry!

The stories of these eighty-eight diverse young men provide an interesting common voice. Eleven major themes emerged from their differing life and faith experiences that describe important crossroads on their way from adolescence to adulthood. In these young men's coming of age stories, the eleven intersections contain a mix of faith and life that shape their emerging identity and their spirituality.

- Relationships: Young men's spirituality is affected by the character, power, and shape of a cluster of significant, primary life relationships. Their families of origin, spouses, current families, friends, classmates, teammates, and colleagues provide a web of belonging and isolation, affirmation and rejection, trust and betrayal, joy and pain that becomes their prime laboratory of faith.

- Male Mentors: Young men's relationships with their fathers and other older male figures emerged as a distinct, significant influence forming their adult spiritual identity. Whether constructively or destructively present, or physically or emotionally absent, fathers were critical factors in these young men's identity and meaning-making. Regularly, other older males became significant surrogate substitute or supplemental "fathers" providing important psychological and spiritual nurture.

- Crisis: A great variety of crises have often been the occasions for the spiritual growth and identity formation of these young men. During these crises, their fundamental beliefs, developing identities, and connections with God and God's people are challenged and most often redefined.

- Life Management: Young men struggle with juggling their time among the competing demands of job, school, friends, significant relationships, and self-care. Their core values and life-orientation are worked out in this struggle for balance in their lives.

- Work: These young men generally find little meaning and purpose in what they do to earn a living. Often their work is a source of stress. Finding meaningful work that is more than just a paycheck or a career about which they are passionate is a struggle, but when it occurs, it becomes a significant element in discovering their place in the world and meaning in life.

- Life-changing Experiences: Young men's spirituality is often shaped by significant events and experiences that reframe their relationships with God and rearrange the many spheres of their lives. These nodal experiences seem to have an especially large impact on their emerging identities, values, and vocations.

- Nature: The spiritual vitality of young men is strongly enhanced by a great variety of outdoor settings and experiences. Many of them spoke about being at peace and of feeling close to God in the mountains, the forest, or on a lake. Many said outdoor activities refresh their spirits.

- Sports: Most young men are enormously kinesthetic. They regularly experience and express their spirituality through bodily action and team collaboration and competition. For many, active or extreme sports are their prime spiritual practices, the means through which they find themselves most alive, connected to others, and at their best.

- Service: Young men are eager to "give something back to their communities" and report a sense of satisfaction and meaning when they do something for others. Although not well formed in their thinking about service to God or changing the world, these actions on behalf of others help these young men "make meaning" and "find significance."

- Avocation: To understand the spirituality of young men is to hear their passions, which are often expressed through their avocations such as music, art, or some other hobby. Most often, these avocations helped them disengage from the stress of their public and private lives. Rarely did they connect these interests directly with their faith.

- Worldly Spiritual Hunger: While not many are institutionally religious, most of these young men experienced a hunger for connection, meaning, and hope that they regularly expressed in non-religious language. Much of their spirituality is focused in humanistic terms and goals. Little of the Christian narrative, especially of the life of Jesus Christ, informs or comes to mind as they speak about faith.

When seen as a network of pathways and crossroads, these young men's journeys and spiritual intersections provide a poignant picture of restless, dynamic humans making their way into adulthood while seeking a vital connection that matters with others, the world, and with God!

Young Men's Voices, Messages, and Our Vantage Point

What follows chronicles the worlds—including the spirituality—of eighty-eight young men coming of age. In the telling of their stories, one can hear them speaking in the midst of changing family, economic, and gender relationships as they come of age, pioneering dynamic and constructive ways of being men. While these young men are not particularly self-reflective, their voices form messages that can be gifts to the church as the church strives to come of age in its ministry with them. The challenge to come of age reflected in these stories is not just a challenge for these young men, but it is also a challenge for the church as it enters more deeply into the worlds and consciousness of these young men as they work out their lives and faith.

These stories present what is true for the young men who shared their lives with us. We hope the telling will encourage the church to "hear into the voices" young men in every community across the country. Perhaps what follows will provide a godly "angle of vision" as to how men might most fully become themselves as unique individuals and common members of the household of faith. The authors suspect that what we discovered to be true of young men regarding spirituality might well resonate with many older men as well.

Structuring the Story

Chapter 2 articulates an "angle of vision" or point of view regarding male identity and gender relationships—a theological and theoretical "angle of vision" that the authors share and found emerging in the coming of age of these eighty-eight young men. This chapter also cites a biblical vision and core values that provide orientation and frame of reference for the church's ministry with men.

Chapters 3 through 9 gather the information shared by these young men, organizing their common voices around seven themes:

- Relationships: Fathers and Male Mentors
- Nature and Sports
- Life-Defining Experiences
- Crises, Stress, and a Balanced Life
- Service and Care for Others
- Work and Avocation
- Spiritual Hunger

These seven themes are developed in each chapter according to the following reoccurring pattern:

- Young Men's Stories
- Summary of Study Findings
- Theological and Theoretical Considerations
- Implications for the Church and Its Ministry

Chapter 10 reflects issues that the authors anticipated would be discovered, yet did not emerge in the lives of these young men. These reflections are included to be honest about some of our biases, to articulate questions for further study, and to engender conversation about the nature of the church and its ministry with young men.

Chapter 11 re-imagines the church's ministry based on what these young men have told us. We experienced these young men to be gifted and eager to realize their potential and call. If the church can connect with their unfolding manhood and engage their hearts, both they and the church will greatly benefit from every young man's search for faith and identity as he comes of age in the presence of the people of God. If the church will listen deeply and respond to these young men in faithful and imaginative ministry, we experienced them ready to stand shoulder to shoulder with each other, young women, and others in the renewal of the church as the church itself comes of age in its life with a new generation.

chapter 2

Young Men and Ministry

Authenticity, Equality, and Mutuality

"Be real, show respect, work together."

Patriarchy's profound shaping of American Christianity has been thoroughly documented. Whether one looks at clergy rosters, surveys the names of denominational leadership, reviews the faces of seminary graduates, or walks through the stacks of theological libraries, the picture is clear: church leadership and teaching have been dominated by men. If one looks over the pews, Sunday schools, church practices, or those carrying out the bulk of service in congregations, judicatories, and church institutions, a very different scene emerges: church life and lay ministry are predominantly made up of women. Male dominance of the church and the feminization of American religion both exist, both have been detrimental to the mission of God in the world, and both call for attention and remedy.

In the last three decades, many in the church have examined its patriarchal character, owned up to its suppression of women, and moved toward the full equality and utilization of women and their gifts. The journey has been painful and often slow and halting. Yet firmly and persistently, women and men are moving toward greater equality and shared capacity for tending each other's gifts and exercising ever more mutual leadership in ministry. Clergy rosters, denominational leadership, seminary graduating classes, and the authors of the books on theological library shelves have changed significantly in the last thirty years. Much has been accomplished; many are engaged in the real work yet remaining to free the church from its male dominance or its "patriarchal captivity."

The Feminization of American Religion

The voices of the young men interviewed in this study issue a call to address the other detriment to God's mission, the gender distortions inherent in the "feminization of American religion." During the early years of the establishment of the colonies in North America, especially in the churches founded by the Puritans, men were thoroughly involved in every aspect of religion, including religious practices and passing on faith in households. By the mid 1800s, great changes had taken place in male participation in religion. Ann Douglas writes in *The Feminization of American Culture*, "The nineteenth-century minister moved in a world of women. He preached mainly to women; he administered what sacraments he performed largely for women; he worked not only for them but with them, in mission and charity work of all kinds . . . the liberal minister began fully to experience his deeper reliance on an audience which was increasingly active, assertive, and feminine."[1] It was not just in presence and numbers but also in influence that American religion was becoming feminized. The English writer Frances Trollope observed, "I never saw a country where religion had so strong a hold upon the women or a slighter hold upon the men."[2]

This shift was celebrated by many who thought it reflected the inherent nature of men and women. Some asserted these alleged inherent differences in men and women as fact and urged that faith be utilized as one of the contributions of faith to overcoming powerful male desires. Eliza Farnham wrote, "The purity of women is the everlasting barrier against which the tides of man's sensual natures surge . . ."[3]

This emerging feminized religion was reflected and communicated in late nineteenth century Protestant iconography. According to Michael Kimmel, "Jesus was commonly depicted as a thin, reedy man with long bony fingers and a lean face with soft, doe like eyes and a beatific countenance—a man who could advise his congregations to love their enemies or turn the other cheek, while gazing dreamily heavenward."[4]

Ministers were to model their behavior after this "Pacific angel." The effect of faith on the lives of men was to mirror this feminine Jesus modeled by the clergy. Kimmel writes of one Methodist minister who described a man's transformation upon accepting Jesus into his life: "It is wonderful to see a great burly man, mostly animal, who has lived under the dominion of his lower nature and given rein to his natural tendencies, when he is born of God and begins to grow in an upward and better direction. His affections begin to lap over his passion. . . . The strong man becomes patient as a lamb, gentle as the mother, artless as the little child. "[5]

Mary Stewart Van Leeuwen, reflecting on this period in American Christianity as a time when the spheres of domesticity (private life) and the public domain became dramatically separated observed, "The result, not surprisingly, is that religion came to be seen as a feminine, not a masculine, pursuit. Throughout the last half of the nineteenth century, white Protestant churches more and more became enclaves for women's activities, and the masculinity of churchgoing men in general, and pastors in particular, came to be somewhat culturally suspect."[6]

Even as this feminization of Christianity continues into our time (the percentage of women to men in attendance at worship has grown steadily from approximately 50/50 to 60/40, and in many cases 65/35 or even 70/30, especially among African-American churches), it has become more subtle while becoming more pervasive. Many of the church's practices of ministry, even the language church leaders use, is more attuned to feminine sensibilities than male realities. Woody Davis cites the following example:

> A pastor friend of mine worked summers on a highway crew during seminary. One day during their break, the seminary student said, "Hey guys, let me share something with you." One man's immediate response was to tiptoe limp-armed through the group saying, "Ooo, we're going to shaaare!" The pastor commented, "I never realized until then how much our church language is feminine. These guys don't 'share.' They tell!" (Woody Davis, unpublished essay)

Some American historians cite the nineteenth century rise of male clubs, fraternal orders, and lodges as a response to the feminization of American Christianity. Together with bars and union halls, these mostly or all male "communities" and organizations became alternative religious institutions—with some even housed in what the members of these secular organizations labeled as "temples."

Muscular Christianity: A Distorted Dead End

An early response to the feminization of American religion emerged at the turn of the twentieth century in what came to be known as "muscular Christianity." The varying expressions of this movement had in common their intention of bringing manliness back into the faith, men back to church, and greater robust Christian influence upon society—especially upon society's "evils." At the heart of this effort was making the image of Jesus more virile and the church more masculine.

These efforts took many turns and expressions. Luther Gulick of the YMCA saw Jesus as an example of magnificent manhood. The movement took a socialist turn expressed in Bouck White's *The Call of the Carpenter,* in which Jesus is depicted as a working class hero and agitator awakening the proletariat. It took a political, racist turn in the Ku Klux Klan where Jesus was portrayed as a "robust, toil-marked young man."[7]

Evangelist Billy Sunday became its most influential proponent. Michael Kimmel writes of Sunday:

> Sunday's mission was the complete transformation of feminized religion, to "strike the death blow at the idea that being a Christian takes a man out of the busy whirl of the world's life and activity and makes him a spineless effeminate proposition. . . ." A Christian cannot be "some sort of dishrag proposition, a wishy-washy, sissified sort of galoot that lets everybody make a doormat out of him. Let me tell you, the manliest man is the man who will acknowledge Jesus Christ." Sunday offered his followers a "hard muscled, pick-axed religion from the gut, tough and resilient," not some "dainty, sissified, lily-livered piety."[8]

All of this came together in the Men and Religion Forward Movement founded by Fred Smith. It was a movement that emerged in 1911-1912 among Protestant churches seeking to bring men back into established religion through depicting a strong, virile Christianity able to take on the evils of society through bold social ministries.

Muscular Christianity exercised a significant theological, ecclesiological, and strategic influence, challenging what was seen as a distorted Christian faith that had skewed the nature of Christ, the power of God, and the character of humanity.

However, in so doing, it responded in an equally distorted fashion, calling Christianity to another narrow range of theological and human characteristics that reinforced patriarchy with its many destructive impulses.

Continuing Dynamics of the Church

Many students of American Christianity observe that the dynamics of patriarchy and feminization remain robust in the twenty-first-century church. Men still greatly outnumber women in the most prominent and powerful leadership roles of American Christianity, especially in the Roman Catholic, Evangelical, and fundamentalist churches. Some of the current men's literature and Christian men's movements either covertly or overtly promote new forms of "muscular Christianity" in which patriarchy is either crassly or subtly present.

On the other hand, women remain a large majority in attendance at worship and in hands-on work in ministry, especially in mainline Christian churches. Regularly, men— especially younger men—are put off by church language and practices resulting in their disengagement from the life and ministry of congregations.

We do not think that American Christianity must always be divided by or oscillate between the "patriarchal captivity of the church" and the "feminization of religion." Inherent in the teachings and life of Jesus Christ is an authentic, egalitarian, and mutual understanding of humanity, gender, and gender relationships. This understanding of humanity and the new creation in Christ (2 Corinthians 5:17) provides a compelling vision for American Christianity and the lives of women and men in the twenty-first century.

We heard a cry for this way of being human in the voices of the young men we interviewed. They wanted life that was true to who they were. They did not want to be something they weren't. Along with this authenticity, they wanted mutuality, to be genuinely connected to each other, friends, and members of their families. They did not want to be connected only with or primarily with men, but with women as well, and with women and men together. They wanted equality; they did not want to be in charge of women or control women. They wanted more than anything else to work out a good relationship with women. Moreover, they saw these relationships as a significant factor in their identity, spirituality, and life of faith.

The young men we interviewed did not want to take Christianity back from women, or to necessarily make it more manly. In their stories and their direct reflections on how the church's ministry might be more effective in their lives, they spoke transparently about their vulnerability, struggles, passions, and gifts. While they spoke specifically about the power of male mentors, they spoke also about mothers, wives, and girlfriends. In all cases, they spoke of the importance of these relationships being authentic, respectful, and trustworthy.

Their voices are a call to the church to come of age, to come to a vision of men and women and the nature and ministry of the church that are authentic, egalitarian, and mutual. A cry emerges from the shared voices of these young men: "Be real, show respect, work together!"

Creation's Original Vision and the New Creation's Vision of Life in Christ

Consider the two Genesis accounts of humankind's creation:

> Then God said, "Let us make humankind in our image, according to our likeness; and let them have dominion over the fish of the sea, and over the birds of the air, and over the

cattle, and over all the wild animals of the earth, and over every creeping thing that creeps upon the earth." So God created humankind in his image, in the image of God he created them; male and female he created them. God blessed them, and God said to them, "Be fruitful and multiply, and fill the earth and subdue it; and have dominion over the fish of the sea and over the birds of the air and over every living thing that moves upon the earth."
    —Genesis 1:26-28

So the LORD God caused a deep sleep to fall upon the man, and he slept; then he took one of his ribs and closed up its place with flesh. And the rib that the LORD God had taken from the man he made into a woman and brought her to the man. Then the man said, "This at last is bone of my bones and flesh of my flesh; this one shall be called Woman, for out of Man this one was taken." Therefore a man leaves his father and his mother and clings to his wife, and they become one flesh. And the man and his wife were both naked and were not ashamed.
    —Genesis 2:21-25

In both of the accounts, men and women are created as distinct persons; men and women are created to be in a distinct, purposeful, and equal relationship with one another. In the first account: the males and females are created in God's image. Together they constitute humankind and, together they are to be "fruitful and multiply" and have "dominion over the earth." In the second account, the male and female are created by God, they are "bone of bone" and "flesh of flesh" (v. 23), they need each other for "companionship" and "assistance," and in their differences they are not to be "ashamed" but to come together to be "one flesh."

Mary Stewart Van Leeuwen, reflecting on these texts, writes, "What is significant here is the shared image of God and the shared cultural mandate. Both man and women were to exercise responsible dominion or stewardship over the rest of creation, and to exercise responsible community by forming families together. But though assigned a set of common tasks, they are clearly formed as two sexes, male and female."[9]

Reflected in both Genesis accounts, gender is a distinction given by God; it is a human dimension bearing the image of God and is a call to shared existence with God, each other, and the larger creation. Gender authenticity, equality, and mutuality as an integral dimension of being sexual, human, and spiritual are at the heart of these texts and constitutive of God's vision for humankind. Again Van Leeuwen writes: "Likewise, sexual complementarity is built into creation as a structure or norm within which persons are to develop the image of God as they engage in responsible stewardship of the earth and create families and communities."[10]

Consider Paul's summarization of the Christian gospel's implications for humankind. In Galatians 3:27-28, Paul writes:

As many of you as were baptized into Christ have clothed yourselves with Christ. There is no longer Jew or Greek, there is no longer slave or free, there is no longer male and female; for all of you are one in Christ Jesus.

In 2 Corinthians 5:17-19, Paul speaks of a new creation:

So if anyone is in Christ, there is a new creation: everything has passed away; see, everything has become new! All this is from God, who reconciled us to himself through Christ, and has given us the ministry of reconciliation; that is, in Christ God was reconciling the world to himself, not counting their trespasses against them, and entrusting the message of reconciliation to us.

In both these accounts of the work of Christ, faith radically changes false distinctions and boundaries, power relations, and their resultant alienations. In Galatians 3, Paul says that God acts in baptism to "clothe" the believer with "Christ." In Christ, boundaries used to divide and exploit fear of and power over the other have no place—and the result is a new integration or oneness. In 2 Corinthians, he proclaims that God acts in Christ to reconcile the world to God's self and calls Christians to this mission. Reconciliation entails no longer separating of or configuring the world on the basis of those who are good or bad, right or wrong. In so doing, radical change has occurred, "everything has become new."

What is God doing with humankind in Christ? What does it mean to be men and women who are "clothed with Christ," who are members of the new creation entrusted with the message of reconciliation? The life of Christ into whom men and women are baptized provides clues.

Christ challenged the barriers between men and women in his teachings and his life. He challenged the competitive, self-righteous definitions of values and power at the heart of his patriarchal society and religion. In the place of these barriers and values, he proclaimed and lived ideals of respect for personal distinctiveness and sacred value; he taught and modeled the power of humility and service; he broke down the cultural barriers between the female private and male public dimensions of life. Both women and men became his followers, workers in his ministry; both men and women were present and reclined with him at the table. He took off has robe, wrapped a towel around his waist, and became domestic servant to those who were at the heart of his public ministry. Jesus got real, showed respect, and called men and women to work together!

According to the apostle Paul, Jesus Christ brings a fundamental challenge to the destructiveness of the distinctions and power allocations of patriarchy. He brings a radical vision of freedom to be authentic in personhood and relationships integrated with responsibility. He issues a call to bring genders, races, and classes together in a partnership to heal the world's alienations. Might sexual identity and gender relationships in this radical vision of the "new creation" (men and women as authentic, equal, and mutual humanity), become a view that incorporates the original vision of Genesis 1 and 2? We believe so.

Possibilities for Life and Ministry with Young Men

The voices of the young men in this study, the Scriptures, and the best of the Christian tradition give shape to a wholesome view of humankind and direction to the church's ministry with men, with women, and with men and women together.

This view of men and women as humankind might well include:

1. The reflection of authentic male and female distinctiveness in social construction and the life and ministry of the church;

2. The enfranchisement of a broader range of constructive human traits, behaviors, and practices for both genders in society and within the life and ministry of the church;

3. The establishment of authenticity, equality, and mutuality for males and females in society and the life and ministry of the church;

4. The development of a unified, interdependent vision of humanity—of men and women throughout society and the life and ministry of the church.

As has been asserted above, there is strong support for these dimensions of the vision in the biblical message.

These basic understandings of male and female suggest that men and women have the freedom and responsibility to discover who they are and who they might become. They have the opportunity to develop all their unique capacities—mental, physical, and spiritual. They have the right and responsibility to find satisfaction not only in nurturing and supporting others, but in being nurtured and supported. They have the right to share equally in making decisions that affect all humankind. They have the right and responsibility to be equipped for mature life emotionally, intellectually, and materially. We found young men hungry for these qualities in their lives.

This vision of gender and sexual relationships might well become language, structures, and dynamics that encourage authenticity, equality, and mutuality for men and women. Language and images promoting opposing visions need to be challenged. Structures fostering injustice, inequality, and lack of authenticity need to be dismantled and reconstructed.

The biblical view of reality is one where authenticity ("getting real"), equality ("showing respect"), and mutuality ("working together") can break forth in language and symbols of God and human character that promote adventure, courage, and action as well as truth, peace, and well-being. The church needs to explore and promote more fully those traits of adventure, courage, and action that fascinate young men. Large dimensions of this work wait to be tackled by biblical scholars, social scientists, linguists, preachers, liturgists, prophets, and caregivers. We hope the stories of these young men will make one significant contribution.

Men and women are not as different as traditional stereotyping would have them be. The differences between females and males need be neither overemphasized nor rendered unimportant. Different chromosomes, anatomy, and hormones are not fully determinative of human destiny, but they affect human existence. Men don't give birth to children. Women don't produce sperm. Men and women's brains are both similarly and differently constructed. Different histories, social conditioning, and societal experiences are not fully determinative of human destiny, but they are realities men and women need to take seriously if they are to be authentic. The young men in this study speak strongly about being taken as they are—in their honesty and authenticity.

Traditionally, sin has primarily exhibited itself as pride in men and timidity in women. Men and women's lives are always contextual and need to be viewed in their concreteness. This emerging vision of gender can be developed into a society and church in which the genuine differences between men and women are discovered and validated. Authenticity, equality, and mutuality can be enhanced by particularity and diversity.

A new vision of gender and sexual relationships can provide language, images, and models that open men and women to their uniqueness without creating a set of male and female superhuman stereotypes. We are led to ask new questions: What are the rich potentialities present in men and women? Which of them make for the good, the right, and the beautiful? How does one encourage the uniqueness of each man or woman? How does the freedom of a unique individual fit with the good of a particular community, church, or society? Each of these questions can be worked by congregations and by Christian people separately in rela-tion to each other. The young men we interviewed seem to be open to explore these questions.

A biblical view of reality commends the importance of the uniqueness, worth, and freedom of each person within the value and necessities of an integrated, interdependent world. Each person is a gift and has gifts for the community. Each individual has need of the community and can be enriched by the community's gifts. Each man and each woman can be free without having to be everything. Each woman and each man can be free to work out their uniqueness in relationship to and be enriched by the uniqueness of others in society and the church. Friendships, marriages, and families can take a variety of forms in providing for basic human needs. Partnerships between males and females can be mutually beneficial while infinitely different. Unique individuals can complement without dominating one another. Individuality and diversity can exist within relatedness and unity.

Therefore, a new vision of gender and sexual relationships needs to be grounded in an interdependent view of reality. Both traditional, stereotypical views of men and women and modern, androgynous visions of persons emphasize distorted views of reality. The first view of men and women and their supposedly vast innate differences, encourages a collusion in which men are dominant and women submissive; the second view blurs their unique characteristics and encourages each person to be autonomous. Neither view is adequate.

The Bible views reality as covenantal. God is the source and sustainer of all creation. The entire created order is connected to the Source who promised never to leave nor destroy it again. Life is based on interdependent patterns and promises. It is grounded in mutual agreements, respectful of all parties, open to renegotiation, inclusive of the full range of life and death issues, and subject to internal and external sanctions. In this view of reality, females and males are unique, of equal value, and mutually interdependent of one another. One can only have individual existence out of one's relationships to others. One can only know relatedness through individuation, which creates a core self from which to be a person. Such is true in the lives of the young men in this study.

In the church, men and women can explore this covenantal view of reality; they can appropriate the compatible notions of individuality and relatedness. A theology grounded in biblical study and the voices of God's present generation can reform our divisive visions and provide a lodestar for men's and women's lives as well as more effective ministry with young men as both they and the church "come of age."

chapter 3

RELATIONSHIPS

Families, Friends, Fathers, and Mentors

We discovered young men deeply influenced by a great variety of relationships. These young men talked about their families of origin, often with delight and passion. They spoke candidly of girlfriends, male peers, mentors, marriages, raising children, in-laws, and extended family relationships. Their stories and descriptions were punctuated by laughter, tears, reflective silence, and an intensity that revealed the seriousness with which they welcomed the exploration of their current life relationships and experience.

Jeremy

Jeremy, age twenty-seven, was active in the church growing up and then again in his adult life. He also quickly identified significant relationships. He is married with three children.

Jeremy notes that a big part of his life outside of work is caring for his girls. He states that "family stuff" gives him joy and satisfaction. His family gives him a sense of serenity that he values highly. He shared an example: "I find peace walking into my daughters' bedrooms and seeing them asleep, curled up in a little ball, and you know they're comfortable. That brings peace to me because they're safe and protected in our house."

Although he and his wife have had their "ups and downs," he credits her with changing his life. A particular challenge in their relationship and his faith was the death of their son, a twin to their oldest daughter. The twins were born prematurely and the boy lived only a day. He describes it as a "tough, tough time." He is not sure how he made it through; he does know he needed the strong support of family and friends. As he reflected about this time in his life, he concluded, "Maybe that's God's answer to me, it's over time. Things do heal."

It is not just his immediate family that Jeremy speaks about. He observes how he works out relationships with both sides of his extended family. "We have our family fights, but we always seem to make up."

With four females in his home, Jeremy is aware of his need for male companionship. He remarks that "women tend to think a little different than guys." He finds the needed male companionship in his father, father-in-law, brothers, and two male work colleagues. The settings for the "guy communications" that Jeremy needs have occurred out-of-doors while hunting or fishing. Jeremy speaks candidly of the importance of those male relationships: "Anytime there's a problem or I have a problem, I always find if I talk about it [with other men], it helps you calm down if you're upset. It tends to help me, anyways, just by talking about it."

Jeremy identifies his grandfather's influence in his life. They explored the outdoors together until his grandfather died in 1996. Regarding his grandfather, Jeremy says, "As a kid we did everything together. He helped shape my life through fishing, going to the cabin, going up to relax and getting away from the cities and helping me find enjoyment, peace, up in the wildlife. He taught me a tremendous amount of stuff." Jeremy noted how his father was part of that same influence in his life. "It would be the same because my father, my grandpa, and myself were always together, did a lot of stuff together."

The church is significant in Jeremy's life. He grew up Roman Catholic and looked up to his priest. It was a "downer" when the priest left, and Jeremy did not attend worship services much after that. It was not until he met his wife that he reengaged with the church. His congregation's unique ministry to families with young children through a program that combined family conversation, prayer, and Bible study with other families was of great help to Jeremy. The program connected Jeremy to the pastor who organized the program. Jeremy feels good that his pastor is "always there for me to talk to."

Jeremy's story combines numerous relationships that have shaped his faith, values, and lifestyle. He identifies three generations of men in his family (grandfather, father and father-in-law, and brothers) who have "been there" for him. Much of his male bonding is linked to hunting, fishing, and the out-of-doors. His wife and children now consume his available time and devotion. The struggles, deep grief, and love expressed for his wife and children are moving tributes to this passionate crucible of his life. Jeremy notes the ups and downs, the connections and disconnects of his experiences in the church. Presently, his church gives him community, support, and training in family life and in the Christian faith that is meaningful.

On the surface, Jeremy's life may look like the 1950s ideal. However, beneath the close family ties and a bond to his congregation are the challenges of a man who has struggled with his marriage, grieved the loss of a grandparent and newborn son, and traversed in and out of a life of faith. It was not until he was welcomed to church through his wife and the opportunity created by his new congregation that he was able to experience, enjoy, and deepen his spiritual life.

Steven

Steven is twenty-seven years old, single, and lives on the West Coast. He grew up in southern California and now lives in the Sacramento area. Steven was raised by his maternal grandparents and moved to live with his mother when he was fourteen years old. He has no siblings. Although he was raised in the church, he is not currently attending any congregation.

Steven is in the process of starting over in a new career after spending his young adult life in banking. He is continuing his education and is a sophomore in college. He is currently dating several women. Steven enjoys relaxing, dancing, going to bars, and playing golf and tennis. He considers himself a "sports fanatic" who can "let it all go," be aggressive, and even "a little mean" on occasion. He watches television news and movies and "plays" the stock market. He is critical of the Internet. According to Steven, there's too much of the Internet. The public has become too dependent on it, and it promotes porn, sexism, and racism.

During Steven's infancy, his mother "hung out with the wrong crowd" and left southern California under a witness protection program. Steven was raised by his mother's parents in Watts, California. His grandfather, a one-time president of Ushers of California in the Methodist Church, was active in the community and traveled to area congregations. Los Angeles Mayor Tom Bradley was a welcomed visitor in their home and on occasion would eat with them. Steven often traveled with his grandfather. His grandfather taught him about life, about being a good citizen, about God, and about how to get along with others. His grandfather was supportive of Christian schools (Steven attended a Catholic school). As a child, Steven was at church four days a week. Both his grandparents were influential in his childhood and early adolescence. From his grandfather he learned to value good citizenship and the Golden Rule.

At age fourteen, Steven lost three friends in gang-related killings. His grandparents decided it was time to get Steven out of Watts, so he was sent to live with his mother in Palo Alto, California. In the move, he went from a relatively low-income family to a life of extravagance. His social contacts were different; he went from a home active in the Christian faith to one where his mother was Buddhist.

Steven is close to his mother and considers her a friend. He admires her Buddhism and Feng Shui philosophy. She has significantly influenced Steven with her nonjudgmental approach to others.

Steven has had many spiritual experiences. When he was a teen, he helped his mother's friend, who was dying of AIDS. The friend had a stroke while in Steven's care and Steven felt God intervened to help him take care of the crisis. Steven sees his life routinely blessed by family and friends.

Steven knows that God is present, intervening for him, and that he will see God one day. Steve believes people need God to make them good human beings. Steven is critical of some in the church who use their positions for personal achievement. For Steven, God is an inner conscience. He prays to God in good times and bad. Steven senses he needs to pray more.

Steven's life and faith have been strongly influenced by two worlds: the world of his grandparents that was deeply Christian and committed to citizenship in a difficult inner city, and the world of his mother with her own distinct Buddhist spirituality living in a more glamorous and wealthy environment in Palo Alto. Steven speaks of good feelings and blessings in helping others and how important his grandparents have been in shaping his faith and values. He said a value

he learned from his grandparents is, "If you have it, give it."
Steven feels most blessed when he helps people. At the same
time, he likes clothes, cars, dancing in bars, and hopes to have
plenty of money to take care of his future family. Steven noted
the fun and adventure he recently had in Las Vegas. He continues to be shaped by the three people most influential in his
life: his grandparents, and his mother.

Jake

Jake is in a different place than Jeremy or Steven. Jake is nineteen years old, lives at home with his parents, is single, and
likes bow hunting, fishing, and big trucks. He sees himself as a
"homebody." He had not been part of the church until recently.
He works forty hours a week waiting tables at a local restaurant.
Jake enjoys taking women to movies and is serious about avoid-
ing "one night stands." His good looks and engaging demeanor
belie shyness and his self-described anxiety in groups.

Jake has spent difficult years in juvenile centers and jail.
He locates the source of his difficulties in his past drinking.
He now attends Alcoholics Anonymous (AA) but finds that it
is not enough. He experiences his greatest contentment and
sense of peace in attending worship services and a church
men's group on a regular basis.

The turning point in his life was his incarceration for drunk
driving. While in jail he realized that something was missing. He was bored and life felt empty. In jail, he met Mark, a
plumber, who regularly visited the inmates. Mark talked about
God and gave Jake a Bible. Mark also taught Jake about the
importance of service to others. Jake describes those times with
Mark as the only times of peace that he had while in jail.

According to Jake, only ten percent of those incarcerated
with him went to church. Through his encounters with Mark, he
realized that he wanted to get connected with a congregation.

While in jail, he also realized that he needed to change friends and that his family—not his friends—was reliable. His experience in jail brought him closer to his parents, to God, and, eventually, to the church.

Jake's first experience in worship after incarceration was a mixed blessing. A woman sitting in front of him was burping her baby when the baby spewed freshly swallowed milk all over Jake. Jake's first thought was this was a bad omen, but he soon interpreted it differently. It reminded him of his past drinking and his own vomiting. It was not a life to which he wanted to return. In worship services he became aware of his inability to carry a tune. He found it comforting that an elderly woman sitting next to him patted him on the hand after a hymn. He took this as a sign of encouragement to keep on singing.

Jake goes to worship alone. He does not have friends or family members who join him. His father attends AA and has been sober for twenty-four years but does not go to church. Neither does Jake's mother. Although they do not join him for worship, his parents are a big part of his support system.

Jake and his father have grown closer since his trouble with the law. Now Jake considers his father his best friend. Jake has fond memories of his father as a hockey coach who understood youth. More recently, his father took him walleye fishing. In the solitude of the lake, he shared with Jake his concerns for him and his drinking. Their time together on the lake changed Jake's life.

Jake gets animated when he talks about his faith. He knows that Jesus and his family have forgiven him for his drinking. He now wants a "full blown, more personal relationship with Jesus." Jake is content going to Sunday worship alone. When he leaves worship, he drives away from the church without his radio on. It is unusual for Jake not to play his radio, but when he leaves worship, he wants to think about the message he just heard. He is not concerned with remembering everything from the sermon. He simply wants to leave with something that he can apply to his life "big time." Jake says he thinks good thoughts when he leaves worship. He goes there to learn something, not simply to "feel better." It is enough for him that his pastor now calls him by name and connects with him after worship, and he attends a men's group once a month. He likes being around "good people."

Jake speaks of his Christian faith changing his life. Jake wants to serve others. Recently, he was able to help elderly women change tires on two separate occasions. Jake understood those occasions as particular blessings from God. He enjoys doing "random acts of kindness," such as visiting his grandmother and giving her a small gift or taking her out for a meal. He often thinks of ways to be kind to people.

Unlike Jeremy, Steven, and many others who were interviewed, Jake does not identify a close family member or friend who has been a direct participant in his spiritual journey. Although he feels close to his parents and welcomes his father's involvement in his life, his parents are not involved in his life in the church. No wife or girlfriend shape his domestic life and there is no ongoing relationship with Mark, the mentor who introduced him to God and gave him a Bible. What Jake does have is a cross-generational worshiping community, where he learns how to apply the Christian faith to his life, and a men's group that he attends regularly. Jake describes himself as one who is comfortable being alone. He is comfortable enough to step into a congregation and be with "good people," know he is loved and forgiven by Jesus, and walk away to be a good person who delights in "random acts of kindness" knowing that "little things make the big picture."

Great Relational Diversity

There is great diversity in the relationships of these young men; there are rich life experiences, passions, and aspirations worthy of attention waiting to be explored. Nearly half of these men (forty-two of eighty-eight) made explicit reference to the central role of their families of origin in their lives. Of the twenty-nine interviewees who were married, twenty-three spoke of the importance, centrality, and delight in their marriages. Four men mentioned that their wives were their "best friends." When children were present in the family, they, too, were often sources of great joy.

Twenty-one men mentioned—sometimes with deep emotion—the roles of their fathers (including step-fathers). In four interviews, the son-father dyad was mentioned as a difficult relationship. Thirty-two men mentioned the significant role of other male mentors. These mentors included grandfathers, uncles, fathers-in-law, coaches, teachers, pastors, scoutmasters, co-workers, and bosses. Twenty-four men mentioned friends (often male) as particularly important to them.

Appreciation for extended family members (including grandparents) was mentioned nineteen times. Fourteen identified other relationships through church or college affiliations as significant. Eleven men mentioned the close relationships they had with their mothers. Eight listed girlfriends as influential in their maturation. (See Figure 1.)

Young Men: The Power of Relationships

Family of origin		42
Male mentors		32
Friends		24
Marriage		23/29
Fathers		21
Extended family		19
Acquaintances		14
Mothers		11
Figure 1	Total in the study	88

These relationships are central to the spiritual life of the young men interviewed. Even for Jake, a "homebody" who is comfortable being alone and who did not mention many personal relationships, the presence of others was central to his faith. Mark, a stranger, entered Jake's life at a critical time during his imprisonment. A smile and a pat from a fellow worshiper were significant. Being called by name and sought out at worship services by his pastor were important. Having a men's group for support was a resource that Jake returns to regularly. Even the recipients of his own care were perceived as important to his faith journey. Relating to, being cared for, and serving others are all components of his faith journey that Jake defined as life changing.

Families

For Jeremy, the role of family relationships in his faith life is clearly evident. Jeremy perceives that his wife was pivotal for his renewed pursuit of faith. His daughters have been a celebrated source of the blessings that God bestows. Even the death of his son and the resultant pain and questioning were occasions for family and friends to step in with support that led Jeremy to affirm God's goodness.

Jeremy's delight in his immediate family is reminiscent of other young men in the study. Jason identified his wife and two young daughters as the greatest sources of meaning, satisfaction, and purpose in his life. He wishes he could spend more time with his children during the week and "lives for vacations and the weekends" with his family. As much as Jason wants to succeed professionally, he sees work simply as a means to the end of support for his family—the most important part of his life. He sees his family in faith terms. He says, "God is obviously an important part of that [family], too. That's why we bring our kids to church, so that we can raise them in the Christian faith."

Jon also spoke of the spiritual life of his home when he described a "picture-perfect moment" in his life. It was the simple pleasure of observing his wife and children on a Friday evening. He witnessed his two children singing, dancing, and playing with their mother and recognized how blessed he was. Other married men with children gave moving testimony to the beauty and joy they have found in their families. More than one man recognized God's presence in his life when he witnessed the birth of his children.

Jim, age thirty-five from California, also exemplified this strong connection to family. His wife and son mean "everything" to him. Jim began to cry when speaking about his wife. He said God blesses him through her.

Dennis is twenty-seven years old and lives with his girlfriend and her son. He expressed a desire to settle down as a family. "Right now, for the first time in my life, the biggest thing that I really, really want to be able to do is take care of [his girlfriend and her son]." Supporting them financially is a huge motivating factor for him and providing for them makes him feel good. "I'm having a feeling of maybe this can be a family situation. I have never actually had that feeling before. Maybe it's just that I'm getting older. I'm looking at it and going, 'Hey, I want to settle down.'"

A common theme found in Jeremy, Steven, and Jake is their admiration for their families of origin. This influence exists across the generations. Daniel, age twenty, mentioned the strong influence of his father, grandparents, and great-grandmother. Other times, as in the case of David, age twenty, the simple category is "family." His family is very important to him. These young men mentioned feeling close to their families or simply being with their families. These family relationships are life-shaping, identity-forming, value-giving, and character-grounding.

Older Men

The young men in our study identified older men who were influential in their lives. Steven did not have a father in his life, but he did have a grandfather who was significant to him. Several other young men mentioned grandfathers as significant people in their lives. In addition to grandfathers, thirty-two of the eighty-eight young men mentioned other male mentors (such as boss, pastor, coach, in-law, friend, or scoutmaster) as significant people in their lives. Although Paul, age twenty-nine, expressed that he has a good relationship with his parents, especially his father, Paul wanted to talk more about Jim, his friend who is fifty-seven years old. Jim is a person who has significantly influenced Paul's life and values. Jim worked for Paul and his wife doing home remodeling and landscaping. Through the work relationship, Jim and his wife and Paul and his wife became close friends. Paul considers Jim a "second uncle." Paul describes Jim as "an extremely nice, giving man." Jim has modeled for Paul the idea of volunteering time to help others work on their homes, share tools, and be very honest and "in your face." Jim is a matter-of-fact person who is loyal and willing to "tell it like it is" when people act irresponsibly. Jim has helped Paul work on his home and yard, and Paul has joined Jim to work on other people's homes and yards.

Fathers

Jake spoke of a powerful and meaningful memory of being on a lake when his father shared "heart to heart" in a fishing boat. Jake took his father's worries for him with deep appreciation and reverence. He described his father as understanding and a person who had been there as an alcoholic and now a recovering alcoholic. Such moments, although not directly linked for Jake with his faith life, are a part of his larger faith and history.

Jake's account of his deep love for his father was replicated many times by other men. This current research notes that fathers make a large and positive impact in the lives of sons. Twenty-one of the eighty-eight interviewed mentioned the positive role of their fathers in their lives. This compares to eleven who mentioned the positive influence of mothers.

The young men who mentioned the positive influence of their fathers often did so with deep affection and respect. Jon talked about his father with tears in his eyes, clearly moved by his father's love, dedication, and sacrifices on behalf of the family. Jon spoke of his deep respect for his father who was widowed early in Jon's life. Although it has only been in recent years that his father could say, "I love you," Jon has known of his father's affection throughout his life. Jon spoke of values he learned at home that included being a good person. He would mention such themes as "Doing the right thing," "Treat others first and treat them well," and "Live a life God wants us to live." Jon describes his father as a "man of faith" and a "stand-up guy." Like a number of other fathers of young men interviewed, Jon's father is a role model for him.

Another example of the powerful faith nurturing relationship between Jon and his father was epitomized on the occasion of the birth of Jon's first child. After two miscarriages, the birth of Jon's first child was a spiritual experience. His father cried when he held Jon's child shortly after the birth. Jon had rarely seen his father cry. That moment left a deep and reverent impression on him. Jon, his wife, his newborn child, and his father, together with the sense of life lived in the presence of a creative, loving God, are significant images in Jon's values and faith.

Spiritual Longings

Families, fathers, and mentors pass on values, beliefs, and lifestyles through speech and action. Relationships offer the "I wanna be like Mike" syndrome—the desire to emulate someone of importance. It may not be the athletic heroism of a Michael Jordan but there is a deep-seated longing on the part of young men to live up to the standards, aspirations, and dreams of those they cherish. Beneath the veneer of casual, off-the-cuff, and often short-lived conversations in day-to-day existence, there is a deep well of devotion to significant others and the faith, values, and character observed in their lives. In those meaningful relationships reside cherished beliefs, faith, values, and a call to courage that makes a difference in the lives of young men. At the root of it all is their pursuit and naming of the very meaning of life.

We walked away from the eighty-eight interviews with a sense of awe and reverence for the privilege of seeing beneath the veneer of these relationships to the depths of these young men's quest for a meaningful life and how they wish to make a difference in an often confusing, challenging, and conflicted world. Beneath the guarded nature of the public life of young men is a spirituality waiting to be explored, clarified, guided, and empowered.

This point is portrayed in the closing comments of Steven. When he was asked for his advice on how the church could connect with young men, he said, "Do this." That is, do interviews that gets young men to open up in a safe relationship to explore the critical, personal issues of life. The interview process offered a relational encounter that served as a lifeline to help them go deeper into their own experiences, values, and wonderment. When Steven said, "Do this," he was emphasizing the importance of establishing relationships with young men, not just programs that seek active, public involvement. "Do this" suggested the more foundational process of getting to know another human being and, in that process, help that human being explore his life. Such conversation is essential to exploring a young man's spiritual longings.

Theological and Theoretical Considerations

As cited earlier, the vast majority of the generation we are studying consider themselves to be believers (79 percent), but these same young people do not have a strong connection to the church (43 percent say they go to church once a month while 32 percent attend once a year or never). According to Craig Miller, "The post modern generation has a healthy skepticism about the church rather than buy into the needs of religious institutions to perpetuate themselves; post moderns seek to make authentic connection with God."[1] He goes on to observe, "For post moderns, belief and attendance at religious services do not necessarily equate." One study concluded, "Sixty percent do not see the church as the best place to pursue their faith."[2] It may be that leaders in the life and ministry of the church who want to connect with post moderns, and especially with young men, will need to redefine "church" and "ministry" for young adults, especially young men.

Redefining church and ministry

While the population of our study was slightly skewed by young men who are currently involved in the life of the church, most of the respondents indicated a faith journey that went beyond the walls of a congregation. The faith, values, and lifestyle of grandparents, parents, and other mentors were everywhere present in the lives of these young men. The sense of awe at the birth of a child, the reverence for a loving parent, grandparent, or other caring mentor, or the influence of a wife were all associated with the presence of a living God in their lives. Sometimes that presence was articulated in the revelation of Jesus; sometimes the description was more generic. No matter how the faith journey was formulated, young men identified God's presence in their lives through personal, trusted relationships, located in their daily lives. This setting of grace needs to be fostered as a major arena for the work of the church with young men.

Dennis names it for himself and for many other young men in the study. Dennis is not connected with the church through a congregation but he is not opposed to exploring the

Christian faith and his own faith journey. He is one of those who says he believes in the "Christian God," but he is not ready to engage in the church, a religious environment that appears to him foreign, uncomfortable, and defensive. He is not in favor of "organized religion," perceiving that various church denominations exist to impose their understandings of what is "right" upon others. While attendance at church "wouldn't attract" him, he indicated an openness to participation in a small group dialog with no conditions or expectations attached. He stated, "The closest that I would come to any religion would maybe be a Bible study or I would enjoy sitting down with one or two people and having a conversation and asking questions and hearing answers and discussing. That, I would enjoy." He enjoys finding out why people think the way they do and would appreciate the chance to converse with Christians, as long as they did not become judgmental. He has been wary of sharing his own thoughts in the past because of the defensive reactions of Christian people. Dennis is looking for an environment that engages people on a more relational and personal than on an institutional and doctrinal basis.

God bearing family life

Biblical evidence suggests that church leaders would do well to see the hand of God at work in people's lives outside of Sunday morning worship, Sunday school, confirmation class, or young adult group. As a Jewish leader grounded in the Hebrew Scriptures, Rabbi Jakobovits describes his own faith tradition by noting that "I belong to a people that trace their origin to the idyllic couples of Abraham and Sarah, of Isaac and Rebecca, of Jacob and Rachel. In other words we are a people who were born at home."[3]

Stephen C. Barton combines the Old Testament tradition of which Rabbi Jakobovits writes with the New Testament witness that speaks of the followers of Jesus as part of a household (Mark 10:28-30) and where Paul uses familial language to describe the believers with whom he works and serves (1 Corinthians 4:17 and 1 Thessalonians 2:7, 11). Barton concludes, "Taken as a whole, then, the Bible is for Christians a book which reveals the true nature of human identity under God, an identity which is explored in the predominantly social-economic-political-religious idiom of marriage and the family."[4] As a consequence, the door to the people of God as conceived in the Bible may not be an entrance to a synagogue or congregation but to friends and families dwelling together in faith, hope, and love. The entrance may well be through primary life relationships.

The larger New Testament appreciation for family life attests to Jesus' view of the religious importance of relationships. When Peter visits Cornelius to present the good news of Jesus Christ, Cornelius does not receive this message in a private audience. He "calls together his relatives and close friends" (Acts 10:24). For this Gentile convert, family and friendship ties are intimately woven into his own reception of the message of Peter. That message is gladly received not only by Cornelius but by the larger community of family and friends. Together they receive the Holy Spirit, are baptized, and continue to mature in this new faith as they invite Peter to remain for several days, obviously to be further grounded in the Christian faith and life (Acts 10:47-48). So essential is the care and attention to family relationships that to not take care of the material needs of family members is to deny "the faith and is worse than an unbeliever" (1 Timothy 5:8).

In Scriptures, both the Old Testament and New Testament, Barton's assessment of the role of marriage and family in faith formation is not restricted to the institutional and programmatic environment of a congregation. The Christian heritage confirms this through the writings and ministry of Martin Luther. For Luther, the home provided foundational and faith-forming relationships. He writes:

> Most certainly father and mother are apostles, bishops, and priests to their children, for it is they who make them acquainted with the gospel. In short, there is no greater or nobler authority on earth than that of parents over their children, for this authority is both spiritual and temporal. Whoever teaches the gospel to another is truly his apostle and bishop. ("The Estate of Marriage," (1522) *LW* 45:46)

Luther gives high honor, in fact, the highest honor, to parents and others who "teach the gospel" for passing on the faith to children. He even gives them the ecclesiastical titles of apostles, bishops, and priests, language usually reserved for institutional church leaders. It is important to note that all who teach the faith are deserving of the title "apostle and bishop." Luther's comment, "Whoever teaches the gospel to another," means that parents do not evangelize alone. They do so with an army of believers equipped with the word of God and loving hearts to spread the gospel and to live lives clothed "with compassion, kindness, humility, meekness, and patience" (Colossians 3:12).

From scriptural evidence and Reformation theology and practice to modern writings and this research on young men's spirituality, the role of family and personal relationships loom large as the means of God's grace. Twenty-seven-year-old Dennis may have more in common with the church than he or we may typically imagine. Dennis' journey of faith follows a path that begins with Abraham and Sarah, Jesus and Paul, Luther and someone who served Dennis as a faith mentor. The question is, "Will leaders of the church today be willing to take the ministry of the church beyond the confines of the institution?" If so, there are numerous avenues the communion of saints can walk with a generation of young men who often remain far from the well-worn path of "church life."

Fathers and other "father figures" as spiritual guides

A second theme in the reflections of our young men is their respect for the lives of parents and other personal mentors (grandparents and close friends). Numerous young men articulated a deep affection for these role models, especially around integrity and honor. The desire to help others was a common theme when reflecting on the influence of these older role models.

Particular attention is given to fathers and other "father figures." Twenty-one of the eighty-eight young men mentioned the specific role that their fathers had in their lives. Others, like Paul and Jake, mentioned men who entered their lives and made a significant difference. Thirty-two of the eighty-eight mentioned male mentors and sometimes multiple male mentors. Rick brought the categories of extended family and other male influence together when he observed, "Pastor is like a grandfather to me." The pastor's personal, non-institutional, non-churchy language grabbed Rick. The pastor had originally introduced himself to Rick with the words, "Wassup Dawg." Rick noted that no pastor ever spoke his language before and he was immediately drawn into a relationship with this pastor who would become for Rick a grandfather figure.

This experience of being mentored by a father figure was expressed well by Jon who spoke of his father's exemplary character and role modeling. Jon used language that was echoed in the comments of other young men about the significant men in their lives. Sometimes with tears, often with deep emotion, young men expressed value and even reverence for the guidance they have received from older male generations. Jon spoke of the guidance he received in language such as "Doing the right thing," "Treat others first, treat them well," and "Live a life God wants us to live." Jon and others could tell moving stories of how fathers and other male mentors had lived a compassionate and honorable life, one that often went unrecognized by the larger society. Being a good person and doing what is right was a common theme. These young men appear to be especially open to the role modeling of dads and elder men. The young men admire and want to emulate the sacrifices and the high standards of truth-telling and honest living, taught through personal, trusted relationships.

Implications for Church and Its Ministry

Church leaders can begin by tending the young men already in their lives (sons, grandsons, sons-in-law, brothers, nephews, co-workers, neighbors, and so forth). Church leaders can listen, affirm, and walk with a generation of young men who are willing to listen, affirm, and challenge in return. There are numerous occasions for mutual respect and mentoring. When given the opportunity for conversation and personal reflection, these young men are passionate, excited about life, engaged in meaningful relationships, and eager to understand the mysteries of life, including life with God.

Listen and converse

Congregations can listen and talk with young men face-to-face ready to hear of their experiences, passions, and aspirations. In order to have meaningful and caring conversations with young men, we need to be with them, that is, join them in public and personal experiences and activities. As we gain their trust, we can have conversations in which we discover their aspirations and concerns. The young men we studied were given personal invitations to be interviewed. Our information was gleaned from young men in the safe and confidential space of a personal interview where there was time for them to be in touch with their feelings and construct their thoughts. Churches can provide ample opportunity for such conversation, listening, and paying attention to the ongoing experiences and passions of young men.

Accompaniment

Congregations can join young men in their living rooms, garages, bike trails, or work places before inviting them to the church. They can be reminded that the sanctuary is not the only place to worship, study, and serve God. Ministries need to be with young men where they are:

- Invite them to lunch and get to know them
- Have coffee or a beer with them
- Fish with them
- Hike with them
- Talk online with them
- Work with them
- Play games with them
- Advocate justice with them
- Advocate on behalf of them

For a possible model of ministry with young men that incorporates listening, conversing and accompanying, see the Appendix.

Focus on young families and relationships

Married young men are focused on family and work. Those who are single tend to have more varied interests and may be searching for long-term relationships and/or a more fulfilling career. Be ready to respond to their family interests and relational concerns with mentoring and small group conversations, as well as instruction in relationships, marriage, family, and parenting:

- Learn about their families and friendships and use what's learned to develop ministry that's responsive to their concerns;
- Ask and respond to questions that do not suggest or impose right answers regarding their relational struggles;

- Equip them to be capable friends, spouses, and fathers;
- Develop a life ministries center that provides counseling and support for young men who need healing and coaching on their way to maturity. (See chapter 11 for such an approach to ministry.)

"God sightings"

Help young men interpret relationships and life experiences as the context of God's work in their lives. Young men are eager to discover God. In fact, they perceive themselves to be religious on their own terms. The church could help young men explore their faith in the safe environment of trusted relationships. Church leaders could:

- Hear the stories of the people in the lives of young men and how those people have influenced them.
- As part of a cross-generational experience with young men (small group study, service project, worship planning, or retreat), ask participants to wonder aloud how their lives were graced by God through the experience.
- Help young men to see God in the midst of daily life. That is, explore with them how God may be at work in their relationships and current life experiences. Help them see that discernment is not only a gift of God for action, it is also a gift of God to help people see the reign of God present among them.
- Provide prayer models for morning, night, and mealtime. With the help of mentors, encourage young men to make prayer a regular part of their lives. Create opportunities for young men to gather and discuss how prayer has influenced their understandings of God's presence and activity in their lives.
- Provide mentors who will on a regular basis discuss and wonder with them how God has been and is at work in their lives.

- In a retreat setting, ask young men to recall and share moments when God seemed particularly present in their lives. Ask on what basis did they have that sense. What was the outcome of that moment? How did it impact or change their lives?
- Form a young men's small group that explores the lives of representative Christian men from the past as possible models for their lives as Christian men.
- Form groups for couples with and without children. Help each group incorporate a life of faith into their family relationships through conversation, devotions, service, and rituals and traditions.

chapter 4

NATURE AND SPORTS

Our young men passionately engage nature and participate in sport. They climb mountains, jam basketballs, lift iron, do martial arts, watch ESPN, cheer their favorite NASCAR driver, snowboard, walk parks, enjoy sunsets, hunt, fish, and hike. The list is endless. Their quest for identity and spirituality is kinesthetic—experienced through their bodies as much as through their minds. With only a few exceptions, this was true regardless of race, class, or context for the young men in our study.

One would think all the activity and energy spent in nature and sports would be recreational, but it is not that simple. Our research shows that most of these young men identify nature and sports as profoundly significant in nurturing and expressing their identity and spirituality. They establish their identity and feed their spirituality with nature and sports activities.

Terry

Bright, articulate, and thoughtful, Terry is wise beyond his twenty-four years. He holds a bachelors degree in international studies and hopes to work at the World Bank. Unlike many interviewed, Terry is exceptionally globally aware. His interest in global issues developed during a year he lived in Norway where he says, "I became aware of global cultures and gained a wider understanding of the world and its people." This experience shapes his future in which he hopes to "effect real change and help cultures get along." Terry is a steel worker and volunteers with the State Department. His work and internship, plus time with his girlfriend and friends, dominate his life. He likes ideas. "Reading churns my mind," he says. Thoughtful and reflective throughout the interview, Terry does not fit the stereotypical jock, yet he is obviously athletic and robust.

As the conversation turned to spiritual matters, a darker mood came over Terry. The son of a pastor, he grew up in the church. Congregational life occupied most of Terry's parents' time and energy, leaving him feeling cheated and neglected. He experienced the tension and hypocrisy that often accompanies congregational ministry. Perhaps, as a result, he identifies integrity, honesty, and authenticity as his most important values.

While not presently active in any church, Terry considers himself a deeply spiritual person. His spirituality is nurtured and expressed in nature and sports. He states that he "feels most human" when he is hiking. "Nature is just how it should be, nature points to a higher power." He links his spiritual fulfillment with kinesthetic activities such as football, rugby, and snowboarding. God is not personal for him and in fact he readily admits, "I don't know [if God exists] and it doesn't bother me that I don't know." He does not worry about matters of salvation. In spite of his agnostic statements, Terry is a deep, spiritual person who nurtures his spirit through nature and athletics. His kinesthetic spirituality nurtures his lifelong desire "to live life as well as I can and to leave the world a better place."

Paul

At eighteen years old Paul is a boyish, high school senior. A sensitive and cerebral young man, Paul enjoys classic movies, physical comedy, German club, snowboarding, camping, hiking, and fishing. He is reflective, curious, and strongly opinionated. Raised and active in the church, Paul has a deep Christian faith. His bouts with depression have driven him to explore and rely on his faith. "God is the one who understands me a whole lot better." His faith is the most important thing in his life and it has been central to him since he was thirteen.

Nature and outdoor activities play a significant role in his identity and faith development. While hiking on Mount Baker he and his group were singing, "Awesome God," a camp song of praise and wonder. Suddenly in the distance, an avalanche broke loose on the mountain and they all stopped and watched. "God was there," he exclaims. Similarly, white-water rafting and rock climbing helped him, "take hold of faith for myself." Soon after the Mount Baker experience he reports cultivating his faith by listening to Christian rock rather than secular music. "It matters what you put in your head," he said. He believes that Jesus is the only way to God and that there are moral absolutes. Through his comparative religious studies, he has concluded that Christianity is "a most revolutionary religion because it's not based upon who you are, rather, it's based upon Jesus and what God is doing."

A Rich Mix

Terry and Paul are representative of nearly all the young men we interviewed, in that nature and sports play crucial roles in developing and sustaining their emerging identity and spirituality. Significantly, neither of these young men is a superior athlete or stereotypical "jock." On the contrary, they are exceptionally cerebral, articulate, and aware young men. They are deep thinkers and surprisingly reflective and insightful.

It is precisely because Terry and Paul do not fit the stereotypical model of the physical male that makes them interesting illustrations of the important role nature and sports play in young adult male spirituality. Our research shows that the vast majority of young men find and give expression to their sense of spirituality and nurture their spirits through kinesthetic and outdoor outlets. Their roots in the creation are experienced through their bodies.

A Metaphor: The Core Experiences

The movie *The Hunt for Red October* is helpful in understanding how bio-neurologically God has "hardwired" young men to need the earth and to express themselves through their bodies in sports. *Red October* is a new, giant, Soviet, nuclear submarine designed with a silent propulsion system. Because it runs quietly, it can get through American defenses undetected and could conceivably launch its missiles on the United States without warning. At one point in the movie, an American submarine, *Dallas*, finds *Red October*. However, when the silent propulsion system is turned on, the giant sub disappears from the sonar screens of the *Dallas*. In his search to understand *Red October's* disappearance, *Dallas's* sonar operator, Jonesy, does a search and analysis of the signal that was lost. The computers report back to him that the only sound they heard was "magma displacement," a reference to undersea volcanic action. Jonesy is not satisfied with this answer. He is aware that the *Dallas* sonar computers were originally designed to read volcanic activity and he is suspicious that when the computer is confused, it returns to its default: "magma displacement." As Jonesy tells his captain, "It sort of runs home to mama." Jonesy begins to review the tapes of the time when the *Red October* disappeared, listening to them at different speeds. He discovers that the sound the computer thinks is "magma displacement" is actually a mechanical sound. With that insight, the hunt for *Red October* is on.

When it comes to young men immersing themselves in nature and sports, they are like Jonesy's computer. When they get confused or are searching for an answer, they find their default form of "magma displacement" in nature and sports. Like the sonar computer, they may not understand all that is out there, but they know where to find home base. Nature and sports often serve as the spiritual home for young men, and it is a source from which they draw great comfort, solace, and inspiration.

So predominant is the role of nature and sports in the lives of these young men that of the eighty-eight interviewed, seventy-three reported this as a strong interest. Eighty-four percent of the young men interviewed in our study turn to nature and sports as a "default response" to cope with life. Of this group, thirty-five percent (thirty-one responses) specifically identify a variety of immersions in natural settings as significant to their lives. In addition, thirty percent (twenty-six responses) report that sports play a vital role while nineteen percent (sixteen responses) report that immersions in both nature and sports are significant to their sense of identity and spirituality.

Looking more closely, we can determine even more nuances in their responses. They do not simply default to their "magma displacement" via nature and sports; they seek one or more of five experiences. Young adult men find in nature and sports: recreation, a sense of peace, identity, bonding, or inspiration. Table 1 below illustrates these five types of responses of the young men in the study.

	Nature	Sports	Both	TOTAL
Recreation	4	9	5	18
Peace	9	0	0	9
Identity	4	13	5	22
Bonding	5	3	0	8
Inspiration	9	1	6	16
TOTAL	31	26	16	73

Table 1

Often these categories overlapped in the interviews. Nature and sports play multiple roles in their lives. One twenty-five year-old Philippino-Hispanic man commented that he is a total outdoor guy, "I like to be out." He snowboards three times a week in the winter, goes river rafting and kayaking in the summer, and loves to go swimming. For him, immersion in nature and sports was both recreational and self-defining.

Twenty-year-old Joseph works sixty hours a week and earns a modest salary. While he is enormously busy, he is excited about playing paintball. "It's very invigorating because it's done outside with lots of running," he said. In the next breath he commented that he liked to do gardening of bonsai trees; it helps him "build patience." Later in the interview, he added that he "feels really alive in nature while camping."

Recreation

Nature and sports provide recreation to many young adult men. Sports in particular serve as a hobby and are often expressed as a passion. They love to watch NASCAR races, attend sporting events, view ESPN, or get in a round of golf.

These young men see nature and sports as play. It is simply fun for them.

Yet, as important as sports and nature are as recreation or as a hobby it would be an error to think that this is the primary way in which they understand these activities. Of the seventy-three responses relating to nature and sports, only eighteen saw this activity primarily as a hobby or recreation. Fifty-five other respondents understood nature and sports at a much deeper level.

Peace

Young adult men turn to nature seeking serenity. They use natural settings such as parks, hiking trails, mountains, lakes, snowmobile trails, sunrises, and sunsets to calm themselves. A few think of these settings as places of escape. They see nature as a way of getting away from it all, as an oasis in life's chaotic desert, and as a hideout from real world pains, struggles and challenges. Others, like Bill who is twenty years old, use nature as a healthy escape. He comments that his most important value is honesty. He wants to be an honest person and expects the same of others. As a result, he reports that he does not always care for his peers much because he "doesn't want to drink my life away." He loves the out-of-doors, especially mountain biking and backpacking. Bill comments that "getting away in nature makes me feel at peace." Bill finds authenticity in nature. Regularly living in the midst of the dishonesty of the party crowd, he escapes into the "realness" of nature. His escape is a search for integrity and truthfulness.

Young men use natural settings as places to think and reflect. Twenty-six-year-old Cory loves the outdoors sitting by a lake or taking a hike. He feels most at peace when in nature. "That's a time when I feel really close to God just because I'm basically there alone with my thoughts and what God created."

Wayne was rebellious throughout his college years, a phenomenon many of these young men reported. "I lived it up a lot and kind of blew what was expected of me. Grades and things like that were not good. So, I kind of blew my chance at that and that was a big blow." He even managed to get himself arrested for "doing something stupid." As he has grown older Wayne has matured and associates a sense of peace with nature. Nature "brings you back to thinking about a lot of different things."

The theme that runs through Bill and Wayne's narratives is the search for authenticity in the peacefulness of nature. Nature is the source and setting for finding what is true, reliable and meaningful. This is a spiritual quest for these young men. Unlike their baby boomer parents who spent their youthful years rebelling against authority, the young male quest is more of a search for authority, for authenticity and for reliability. Even those who became the "wild child" in their late teens seemed motivated more by life's temptations or by personal hurt experienced in their upbringing than rebellion. Their parents spent years pushing against or away from the older generations and the norms of society. While occasionally rebellious, the young men seemed to be reaching out and grabbing onto something they could count on. The motion and flow of their parents at this age was to move out and away, like a bird leaving a nest, while the motion and flow of these young men seems to be longing for a nest to which they can be anchored. Many find that nest in the wonders of nature.

In her book, *Big Questions, Worthy Dreams,* author Sharon Daloz Parks shares a letter written by twenty-three-year-old Mark. His words eloquently capture how nature plays a vital role in the young adult male spiritual quest as a source of peace, authority, and place for nesting.

Just today I have finally realized that I am sitting right on top of my spiritual teacher: the Earth generally but, more specifically, this mountain. A mountain is the perfect teacher. It can teach you everything you need to know about living. It does not try to humble you or force you to bow down before it, but it absolutely demands respect. When you are on a mountain, you need to be there body and mind. You can't take the mountain carelessly or too lightly. It has the immediate law of karma, or responsibility for your actions. If you are careless and step in the wrong place the mountain may decide you would be happier in the valley and it will send you there.[1]

It is significant that active sports do not play the same role of creating a sense of peace. No respondents thought their sports activities gave them the serenity that nature does. Whereas engagement in active sports doesn't quiet them, they do find in sports opportunities to think and reflect, especially regarding their identity.

Identity

Young men use sports to define themselves, often in the crucible of competition and challenge. They do this more often than by immersing themselves in nature. They eagerly seek this engagement and the testing it provides. Twenty-seven-year-old Scott said of sports, "It's where I can let it all go and be aggressive and mean." In addition to discovering who they are through sports, they use the competitive nature of sport for centering or to focus their purpose and place.

Sports are an important part of Peter's self-identity. Peter has a passion for sport and "can't get enough of it. It kind of drives me," he reports. "I love competition. If I didn't have it, my life would be a lot different." Peter is involved in track and football.

Like Peter, Craig sees physical activity as important to his identity. At thirty years old, Craig works fifty-five hours a week as a teacher, baseball coach, and fitness center director. For personal and professional reasons, he stays fit, but working out also has a spiritual dimension for him. Exercising alone (running and weight lifting) "gives me a lot of time to think. . . . When I'm working out, I like to really push myself, and you get down to some points in a workout where you have to really fight through and that really causes me to focus on myself. And then during the rest periods, I think about my thoughts. That's when it really gets me. I do some spiritual growing in those sessions. . . . When it's just me I can do a lot of thinking. I think it's good for me. . . . I think about where I'm at in my life right now and what role that God plays in those areas." Craig continues, saying that playing competitive sports "helps me to learn more about me and really helps me to find out some things about me that are deep down. Anytime you can learn about yourself, I think there's a spiritual aspect to that."

Both Peter and Craig are literally physically in the process of forming their identity. This is an important dimension of the young male quest. Most of these young men "act into," or kinesthetically derive their sense of self. They naturally and healthily integrate their thinking process with their bodily activities. They do not separate themselves into body and spirit. Rather, they instinctively hold body and spirit together in their quest. For most, their bodies are often the means by which they address larger issues of place, purpose, meaning, and truth. In the physical activity itself, they can "think their thoughts." Through their physical activity comes mental processing, personal reflection, cognitive development, spiritual focus, and insight.

Bonding

The young male spiritual quest includes the development of social bonds, especially with other males. This is not simple, since males seem less neurologically developed for making empathetic social connections than their female counterparts. (For more on this subject we suggest reading *The Essential Difference* by Simon Baron-Cohen.) How and with whom males bond will often involve an immersion in nature or sports.

Dan, at age twenty-six, is working on an MBA degree. He is single and earns a good living in finance. On weekends, he enjoys football and softball. He is a booster of the local university football team and, as a season ticket holder, he spends his weekends supporting the university and flying to games with friends. A great part of his social network is found among the university football boosters. Dan reports that the significant events that shaped his life involved his grandfather. His grandfather took him to football games. They went fishing and hunting, and they went to church together. Dan speaks fondly of two of his best friends, who are also active in sports. Dan states his priorities: first, job; second, having fun hunting, fishing, and following football; third, God; and fourth, parents.

Hal's significant bonding experiences are similar to those of Dan. At thirty-three, he is the father of two girls and does well in sales. He is a former golf pro. He reports that his most significant bonding experiences took place with his father and grandfather playing golf or going fishing. In keeping with these family traditions, he loves to take his two girls fishing, hiking, and camping.

Dan and Hal both illustrate the vital role that nature and sports play in male bonding. These young men did not form bonds sitting in circles talking. They converse and connect while acting. Immersions in nature and sports often serve both as context and content for male bonding.

Inspiration

Nature inspires these young men. When we asked them the question, "What makes you feel really alive?" they most often responded: "a significant relationship or moments in nature." Nature gives them energy and provides a sense of awe for them. Their spiritual quest has a cosmological character to it. They speak like the psalmist who said,

When I look at your heavens, the work of your fingers,
the moon and the stars that you have established;
what are human beings that you are mindful of them,
mortals that you care for them? (Psalm 8:3)

Randy is twenty-four years old and is attending college after serving in the Navy. His parents are divorced, a divorce that was hard on him. Besides the emotional loss of the divorce, it left him impoverished during his junior and senior high school years. Boot camp and a stint aboard a U. S. Navy ship were hard for him as well. Although difficult, Randy notes that boot camp was a spiritual experience. Randy feels alive when he is surfing and feeling the wind. "Being in Mother Nature and doing athletic stuff makes me feel alive." He had the same feeling when at sea with no flight operations and calm seas. He notes that when he walks the decks and watches the sun set and sees the birds and the water, he feels connected and alive.

Newly married for a second time, Ricky works in an architectural firm. At age thirty-three, Ricky, like so many others, struggles with finding enough time in the day. After college he struggled with direction. His church attendance waned. His divorce was exceptionally difficult. Dealing with divorce drew Ricky back to church. "I'd say faith got me through it. While it was a tough time for me, I never gave up on God," he said. As a part of his recovery, Ricky loves camping, backpacking, fishing, and hunting. Being in nature energizes him and affirms his belief in God. "Seeing God's creation just makes me appreciate life. The majesty of mountains makes me think 'this is beautiful, this couldn't just happen from a big boom.' God had to make this."

Ricky, Randy, and the psalmist reflect the vital role that the awe and wonder of nature can play in a spiritual quest. Bob says that the mountains and the ocean give him a sense of being alive. "Nature invokes in me a sense of the 'awesome' and appreciation of God as the great giver," he said. All of these young men reflect a creation-based theology. They are excited and moved by the cosmos. Some of these young men are more pantheistic in their thinking (God is the mountain), while others interpret the natural vistas in more deistic ways (God made the mountain and now is far removed).

The nuanced depth of young men in the interpretation and utilization of nature and sports is multi-layered and multi-faceted. We have identified multiple functions of nature and sports in their lives that overlap and often work in concert. Like parfait ice cream, these applications swirl in and around one another creating a kaleidoscope of color and flavors. For purposes of analysis, we have pulled them apart. In the real world of young men, they are stirred together in a rich blend. In ministry with these young men, the church dare not ignore the importance of nature and sports in their spiritual questing. This analysis begs the question: why are nature and sports so vital in their spiritual quest? It is to this question we turn next.

Theological and Theoretical Considerations

In the winter of 2002, a group of young seminarians studied outdoor ministries. There were eleven people in the course, five men and six women. Following a long day of travel, the class finished dinner in a camp dining hall. At one end of the dining hall was a large fireplace with a warm, crackling fire. At the other end was a foosball table. Within two minutes of cleaning the dishes, all five young men congregated around the foosball table and began hammering the ball with their players, screaming and cheering loudly, challenging and taunting one another playfully and competing aggressively. The women pulled up the couches and gathered around the fire for an evening of quiet conversation.

Why do immersions in nature and sports play such a large role in the spiritual quest of young men? The short answer is that from the time of their conception, most males have been genetically programmed to be more kinesthetic beings. Many mothers report their boy babies kicked more in the womb than their girl babies. Nursery care providers report that if several female toddlers and a single male toddler are playing in a common space, the male toddler will use up more of the space than all the females. Public schools report that ninety percent of the problems they experience come from boys and that boys are more aggressive, active, and kinesthetic than girls at every age level. Boys differ most significantly from girls when it comes to the need to move, act, wiggle, and compete.

Some would take exception with generalizing these differences. There are significant differences between males and females. However, we want to be clear that biology is not destiny and brain differences between males and females should not be used to justify sex stereotyping or discrimination. In addition, within any population of males and females reside the glorious variety and differences of humanity as God intends. We know young women who value sports and nature as much if not more so than some men. Thanks to the feminist movement and the passage of Title IX legislation, women are immersing themselves in sports in ways that cultural barriers prevented in the past. In this process, young women as well as young men are engaging in a "kinesthetic spiritual" quest. Our intention is not to exclude women from sharing the same ground as these young men but to describe what we have found to be true of most of the young men in this study. In addition, even as some young women would fit this profile and some young men would not, we argue that it is very likely that young adult males will self-identify nature and sports activities as playing a large role in their spiritual quest. One of the reasons has to do with the way their brains function.

From the time of conception, male brains are more oriented toward kinesthetic activities such as sports and nature. Scientists have identified fifty-five hormones that play a role in shaping human beings, but it is the male hormone testosterone that makes a most significant difference for men. Within the womb and throughout life, especially during puberty and young adulthood, testosterone surges through their systems and shapes the brains of males. Testosterone is the hormone of aggression. It enlarges the muscles of males, stimulates competitive and aggressive male behavior, and fires the sex drive of males. This process begins as early as six weeks after conception when the genetic code introduces testosterone into the fetus thus forming a male brain and body.

At puberty, testosterone levels within adolescent males surge to more than two hundred times the levels found in girls. These surges of testosterone can occur seven to ten times a day. Young men produce one thousand sperm per second. Their voices change, their bodies grow up to eleven inches in one year, and their moods can turn dark, surly, and aggressive. Men often take risks that make no sense, they regularly compete and challenge their peers and primary adults, and between long naps and giant meals they seem to be a perpetual motion machine. Most significantly, their brains are exploding in growth in ways seen only when they were infants.

For more than four millennia, humanity has recognized that young men are different than their female counterparts. These differences require careful attention lest young men become destructive. The Spartans of the Greek city-state placed their young men in the military and put them through rigorous training. Aristotle encouraged all young men to explore, survey, and memorize the territory of Athens. He believed the government should pay for such training for all young men. The Romans gave their young men their own god, Juvantes (the source of the word "juvenile") and developed their young men as warriors and explorers, as well as scholars and politicians. Throughout the Middle Ages in Europe, many young men aspired to become knights who defended land, country, and faith. During the industrial revolution, Christians concerned about the temptations of urban life developed the YMCA to positively engage young men. These programs were evangelical and kinesthetic. The Boy Scouts were intended to serve the same purpose from a secular perspective. Since the late 1940s and early 1950s, we have seen a rapid growth of camps, retreat centers, and nature preserves developed by churches, government agencies, schools, and colleges that offer nature and sports outlets for males and females alike.

Historically, cultures have known males think differently than females but until recently have not known why. Recent developments in brain scanning technology, such as the functional magnetic resonant imaging machine (FMRI) are helping unravel the mystery. Scientists can now watch a brain working and see the differences on a monitor. What they are seeing is that the young male brain functions differently than the female brain. Most males use the right hemisphere of their brain more than their left. Testosterone shaped their brains to work this way from the very beginning. The right hemisphere of the male brain develops first in boys while the opposite is true for girls.[2] In addition, females utilize both hemispheres of their brain simultaneously whereas males generally access their right hemisphere and only intermittently their left hemisphere.

The right hemisphere of the brain is the "novelty center." It is the place where the human brain orientates itself spatially. The right hemisphere of the brain utilizes images more than speech, action more than stillness. It is the creative brain that generates risk, spontaneity, and creativity. The right side of the brain is "adventuresome." It seeks stimulation and competition and physical manipulation of the world.

The right hemisphere is the pre-verbal brain. It does not put things into words; rather it creates images and actions. This, in part, explains why adolescent and even many young adult men have poor verbal and reading skills. It also helps explain why ninety percent of pornography is watched by males and young males in particular. Pornography stimulates the right hemisphere of the brain as well as the testosterone saturated hypothalamus, those parts of the brain having to do with sex and the sex drive.[3]

The male brain makes verbal communication difficult because of the *corpus callosum*. This part of the brain joins the two hemispheres and is ten percent smaller in males than females. This neural mass is designed to move the experiences of the right hemisphere into words through the left hemisphere, especially the left temporal lobe. It is generally thought that because the *corpus callosum* is smaller in males than females, males have less biological capacity to develop verbal communication.

The following conclusions can be drawn from this brief exploration of the brain:

- Young adult males are biologically structured to seek and embrace the kinesthetic activities of sports and nature.

- Young men are drawn toward visual images of God such as those seen in nature as opposed to verbal images of God such as those in a sermon.

- Young men have a biological tendency to define themselves through competitive, aggressive activities such as those in sports and personal, physical challenges.

- Young men are predisposed toward finding peace in dramatic visual images such as those found in natural settings.

- Young men have a biological tendency toward active recreation, including computer games, since these are right brain, spatial, and physically manipulative activities.

- Young men have a biological inclination to bond with one another through immersions in nature, sports, and other kinesthetic activities such as car repair, construction, or a project.

- Young men are inclined to seek inspiration, truth, and authenticity through visual and spatial means such as those in nature and the intensity of sports.

- Young men are inclined to make their spiritual quest through nature, sports, and kinesthetic activities.

In our reference to the movie *The Hunt for Red October* Jonesy's sonar computer had a default orientation of identifying "magma displacement" as response to situations it did not fully understand. Like Jonesy's computer, young men have a default orientation driving the way they think and process life, shaping the way they seek answers to the challenges and mysteries of life. Part of that default orientation comes from their right hemisphere thinking, thus finding recreation, peace, identity, bonding, and inspiration in frequent and intensive immersions in nature and sports.

We have seen the manifestation of young adult male brains embracing nature and sports. These young adult men are, by nature, "creation theologians." They are most likely to identify with and understand the First Article of the Apostles Creed, "I believe in God the Father almighty, Creator of heaven and earth." In the beginning of this chapter, we spoke of Terry, the globally aware, congregationally disenchanted steel worker. He summarizes our point, "Nature is just how it should be, nature points to a higher power." Paul also demonstrates this creation theology when he saw the avalanche on Mt. Baker and observed, "God was there."

This is good news to Christians reaching out to young men. Christianity is an earthly faith. Jesus became incarnate as a physical, tangible, real human. Humans have seen God, heard God, and even touched God (in baptism and the Lord's Supper), and known Jesus' presence in his life and work. Recall that the apostle Thomas demanded, "Unless I see [right brain] the mark of the nails in his hands, and put my finger in the mark of the nails and my hand in his side, I will not believe"

(John 20:25). Once Thomas touched Jesus, he came to faith. He typifies a young, male believer.

Christians might well portray this "material Jesus" to young men because visual and physical outlets and natural settings are such critical access points in their spiritual quest. Like many of those we interviewed, Jesus makes a journey similar to theirs when he enters the wilderness for forty days (Luke 4:1-13). Here we find God incarnate wandering in nature, amidst the mountains, valleys, deserts, and rocks. He is physically challenged and pushed to his limits lacking food and water. Power, material wealth, and false worship are laid out before him. At this moment, Jesus confronts issues that many young men are facing.

Some of these young men went through a "wild child" phase of life. They engaged in reckless living, conspicuous consumption, and abuse of their powers. They are like the prodigal son, who after a wasted life, "came to himself" [right hemisphere connection with the left hemisphere?] (Luke 15:17). Jesus works these issues in nature under extreme physical and mental challenges. This Jesus of the wilderness could strike a familiar chord with the young male spiritual quest. The question for ministry with young men is whether this is the Jesus that is being presented to them.

The critical point is that by using language, metaphors, and stories of nature, and including kinesthetic activities in ministry, young adult males are more likely to "get it." The stories of Samson, Jacob's wrestling with God's messenger, the many stories of Jesus' healings, even Jesus' cursing of the fig tree are earthy, kinesthetic, physical, and pictorial narratives that might connect well with young men. They might better grasp the Scriptures and claim the gospel if we do not so much speak as act out and visualize the story in ways that address their right brain thinking. This means that it is vital to link the good news of Jesus Christ with their quest for recreation, peace, identity, bonding, and inspiration through immersions in nature and sports.

Implications for the Church and Its Ministry

One of the strangest and most insightful experiences we had while doing this research took place in North Carolina. Our hosts in the congregation's men's ministry had arranged an interview schedule in their congregation. As we set up for the day, the parking lot was full of pick-ups carrying wood chips, plants, shovels, ladders, and carpentry tools. Our hosts informed us that this was the men's day to maintain and care for the congregation's grounds. The plan was for us to interview the young men while the older men (ages forty to seventy) worked. Later, we'd all have lunch together.

At mid-morning it rained. During one of the breaks in our interview schedule, Paul went to visit the older men and found these men working, laughing, and playing in the rain. They looked like fifth-grade boys stomping in a creek. The women of the congregation stood at the doors and commented on how stupid this looked. The men, "boys," the women called them, were in nature, navigating the challenges of a rain storm, pulling together, and energized by the task. The rain only enhanced the experience.

One of the young men interviewed stood at the entrance and said, "I just joined this group." Paul saw the look in the young man's eyes and knew the young man thought what was going on was "cool." During lunch, the men regaled one another on their adventure dripping puddles on the gymnasium floor, pausing to listen to the rain on the roof. This is effective men's ministry.

The young men had suggestions regarding ministry strategies using nature and sports. Following the five functions of nature and sports identified earlier, below are examples for an effective ministry with young men.

Recreation

- Build or rent a gymnasium.

- Host or join a sports league: summer softball, midnight basketball, or computer gaming. Some of the best ministry with young men happens while playing left field on a church softball team.

- Establish a local chapter of the Fellowship of Christian Athletes.

- Attend the sports events of the members of your church and create your own church fan club.

- Create a weight and exercise room in your church building.

- Use a golf outing as a congregational fund-raiser and charge a dollar for every stroke. Use these funds to send youth to camp.

- Create an archery range on the church campus before bow hunting season.

- Start a coed congregational swim team.

- Offer free or partial memberships to local gun clubs so that young men can learn safety procedures.

- Offer martial arts and self-defense classes in your church. Karate clubs are looking for space for their classes. Congregations often have some good space that can be utilized.

- It seemed like everyone we talked to said, "mountain bike!"

- Add Bible study conversation and prayer.

Peace

- Work through the life of Jesus utilizing the gospels and media depicting Christ's life. Do so on retreats in natural settings.

- Create contemplative spaces with plants, gardens, and fountains in the church building or on the congregational grounds.

- Build a brick labyrinth on congregation property.

- Hold small group devotions in a quiet cemetery.

- Do stargazing. Some studies show that nearly eighty percent of all youth have never seen the night sky.

- Go camping together.

- Develop a Bible study series on the stewardship of creation. Hold it in a natural setting.

- Provide childcare so that young couples can go hiking, running, biking, or exercising together on weekends.

- Provide copies of the Psalms that focus on nature for these young men when they hike in parks, forests, mountains, and other natural settings.

- Provide sunrise and sunset devotions, such as morning and evening matins, in the worship resource, *With One Voice.*

- Create a campfire site on the church property.

Identity

- Publicize the sports performances of members of your church with news clips on your church Web site, as well as on the bulletin board.

- Ask young men to demonstrate a sport or nature activity and involve others—especially younger boys.

- Integrate a Bible study on God's call and vocation into a sports outing or immersion in nature. Certainly, the story of Jesus' challenges in the wilderness would be appropriate.

- Get to know Christian farmers.

- Find out who the professional Christian athletes are in your area and invite them to speak at your congregation.

Bonding

- Take a cross-generational group of men on an adventure trip or retreat. Many of the young men spoke fondly of the group cohesiveness that came from a backpack or canoe trip.

- Build a skateboard park. We were surprised at how many of these young men skateboard into their late twenties.

- Help groom and maintain cross-country, ATV, and snowmobile trails as a service and witness to the larger community.

- Participate in a Habitat for Humanity project.

- Develop a Saturday morning running or bike club. Have breakfast and a Bible study after the workout.

- Create a climbing, swimming, canoeing, boating, car, or computer club, event, or ministry.

- Form a Weight Watchers group and hold one another accountable through regular exercise, Bible study, and diet.

- Create your own "Christian Sports Cafe" for Monday night football and Super Bowl Sunday.

- Establish an environmental protection group. Adopt a segment of highway or a portion of a waterfront and keep them clean.

Inspiration

- Incorporate illustrations, metaphors, and stories that come from the world of sports and nature into preaching and teaching.

- Go to an outdoor ministry facility for a week or retreat weekend.

- Hold a worship service for hunters and fisherman before the opening of the season. Emphasize the stewardship of creation.

- Hold worship services outside—all summer if possible.

- If you are a Christian farmer, invite young men to your land and speak of your sense of call.

- Visit Mt. Saint Helens.

chapter 5

LIFE-DEFINING EXPERIENCES

Martin Luther, Buddha, and Muhammad are world religious leaders that were deeply influenced and shaped by life-defining "nodal experiences." As a young man, Martin Luther entered the University of Erfurt in 1501 intending to become a lawyer. However, in 1505, Luther's life took a dramatic turn; he entered a monastery and became a priest in 1507. He later became a professor at the University and in this role, served as a catalytic agent for religious, cultural, and social change in the Western world. What altered Luther's life was a "nodal experience."

While preparing to be a lawyer, Luther was caught up in a ferocious thunderstorm as he was travelling in the countryside. He was terrified by the experience and in his panic cried out, "Help me, Saint Anne, I'll become a monk." Luther interpreted his escape to be the work of God. He kept his vow, entered the monastery, and the rest of the story is the Reformation.

Like Luther, Siddhartha Gautama (Buddha), began his life as a young man on one course, only to go in a completely different direction. Born between 500-400 B.C. Gautama grew up in the foothills of Nepal. The son of a warrior prince, he lived his early years in luxury, he was married at twenty, and fathered a child. At the age of twenty-nine, Gautama had four visions that convinced him to leave his family and seek religious enlightenment. For six years he wandered, practicing extreme forms of self-denial. Finding little satisfaction or insight in these practices (much like Luther's early years in the monastery) he meditated under a shady bodhi tree. Suddenly, he came to enlightenment concluding that the way to peace and happiness (*nirvana*) was to become free of all desires. This nodal experience under the bodhi tree changed Gautama into Buddha.

Raised by his extended family in the deserts of Arabia and Syria, Muhammad married into wealth at the age of twenty-five. While meditating alone in a cave he had a vision of the angel Gabriel who called him to become a prophet and proclaim God's message to the people. At first, uncertain of this calling, he told people of his experience, many of whom rebuked him. He fled from Mecca to Medina where he was warmly received and his leadership took root. He became the voice for a religious and cultural life that dominates a large segment of the world's population. In the cave, Muhammad had a nodal experience that changed his life and the world.

All three of these giants of history experienced nodal moments while in their young adult years. As a result, they became different people with new focus on life and a deep sense of purpose and determination. Their stories are dramatic representations of what we heard in less dramatic form from sixty-three of the eighty-eight young men that took part in our study. God continues to shape young men through powerful and transformative events.

The dictionary defines nodal as "a knot or complication in the plot or character development of a story."[1] A "complication of the plot of a character" is a way of saying one's life is interrupted so dramatically that one can no longer be the same. These interruptions took many shapes and forms in the young men in our study. We will describe five types: immersions, sufferings, competencies, family events, and mentoring. What makes these nodal moments is that the young men experiencing one or more of them are transformed by the experience. Their personal character is complicated, interrupted, or challenged in such a way that their lives take new directions even as they have become different and more reflective human beings.

We define nodal experiences as "unplanned, personal interruptions or events in the lives of young men that dramatically and positively alter and transform their understandings of God, themselves, and the world." It is important to emphasize the positive nature of these experiences. Nodal experiences are the means of the Holy Spirit working in these young men, broadening their perspectives, and in some cases deepening their trust in God. These experiences are usually unplanned. They occur serendipitously, often surprising both the young men and those alongside them. Our research shows that of the five types, the two most significant nodal experiences affecting these young adult males are immersions and sufferings.

Immersions refer to experiences where the young man is removed from his normal setting and placed into another context, such as a camp or retreat. Immersions also include mission trips, travel experiences, and group gatherings. Besides separating the young man from his regular routine, the immersion generally takes place over an extended period of time.

David

David's two immersion experiences are representative of the forty-eight responses that illustrate this category. David is

---

thirty years old and teaches behavior management classes to troubled adolescent youth. David and his wife are expecting their first child. He is physically and emotionally close to his parents. He considers his family relationships to be very important. Whereas he grew up active in the church (he and his wife are both pastors' children), he drifted away from the church after college. "My involvement in the church as a child and teenager had been largely social, and I found other outlets for that as a young adult." Moving to a new community has rekindled interest in David and his wife for a faith community. "We are feeling like now we are adults. I've turned thirty and we are going to have a baby. We bought a house so church is something we are supposed to do right? I've gone through periods of time within the last six months where I really feel like I want to go to church. I wake up and I want to be there." David is describing the nodal experience we are calling "family events." However, as we hear more, we discover the power of immersions in his life.

While in high school, David had the opportunity to travel to Germany. He has subsequently made a number of trips there. "To see life in a different country was 'huge' for me. It helped me to see that the world is bigger than my surroundings and made me grow tremendously."

David's other immersion nodal experience took place at a summer church camp. In fact, we received nineteen responses relating to nodal experiences taking place at a camp or in a retreat setting. "I had the experience of doing the summer camps as a kid, and then went back to work as a counselor and do that whole bit. I think I felt more connected to God sitting out in the woods with twenty kids and just talking about 'what do you think this means, do you think that this whale really swallowed this guy and cruised around and then he was all fine and he was spat out, or is there something deeper that we should get out of this?' I think I felt more connected when we were just sitting out having conversation and letting people tell you what they think and you tell those people what you think. To me that was it!"

Although no one can fully measure the impact of David's travel and camp immersions, they obviously have significantly shaped him. They led him to reflect upon his life in the light of Scripture. As a part of the reflection he has renewed interest in a faith community.

Ricky

Suffering is another type of nodal experience identified in our research. Sufferings refer to either self-inflicted or externally perpetrated experiences which cause the young man to struggle and experience pain. We recorded twenty-nine accounts of this type of nodal experience.

Ricky's story is illustrative of sufferings. At twenty-nine, Ricky is a body shop manager married with three children, including a daughter from a previous relationship. His wife works full-time, thus Ricky describes his lifestyle as "fairly busy." In fact, Ricky's biggest current struggle is achieving balance between all that he has going and not getting burnt out or neglecting the people who are important to him. Ricky's family means everything to him. "Just coming home and having everybody there, being able to sit down and share the day and talk with each other about things, seeing the kids grow and develop; it's neat just to sit there and be with everybody, to be all together."

Ricky's biological father has been virtually absent but his stepfather has been there for him since he was six years old. During high school, Ricky was "relatively trouble free." He gained acceptance into his preferred college, which was "a big high" for his family. Upon going to college, Ricky says he "lived it up a lot and kind of blew what was expected of me, grades and things like that were not good. So I kind of blew my chance at that, and that was a big low." He returned home to live with his parents and attended a community college. He moved in with his (now) ex-girlfriend and they had a child together. When his ex-girlfriend became engaged to another man, they isolated Ricky from his daughter. A messy court case ensued. At the same time Ricky moved in with the woman who is now his wife. They had a son and later were married. Ricky describes this sequence of events as "a very harsh thing that happened."

Coupled with these sufferings, Ricky was arrested during his first year of college because of "doing something stupid," as he said. "I for sure thought that was going to be a big deal, a big problem. I called and let my mom and dad know. I felt real bad about it. My dad showed up at the jail. I didn't have to go to court, and they dropped the charges. My dad was there when I walked out of the door and he was there with everything that was needed—a lawyer, cash, or whatever to bail me out. That was really a firm kind of a beginning again in my life, in my relationship with my dad, because it didn't seem like we were just kind of there together, we were father and son. It was really important that he did that for me and he didn't ask questions, he did nothing, just came and picked me up and said, 'Let's go home. Can I get your truck and get your stuff and let's go home?' That was real, real important in our relationship, that was a real turning point." Ricky now considers his father a key confidant and source of advice for him.

Reflecting on his adolescent and young adult years, Ricky notes that his family attended church regularly but following confirmation, he was not involved. He explored all his questions and doubts. His next point of contact with the church came with the baptism of his son before he got married. The baptism was held at his parent's church. "We knew we wanted him baptized, but I don't think we knew really why or anything." When his family moved to a new community, they felt the need to join a church. "We just felt we needed to go and we found it was just a great place to be. It's a big church, lots of people, lots of things going on. Finding this place is a big high."

Ricky's chaotic young adult years are typical of the stories we heard. Nearly all of his pain and suffering during this time was self-inflicted. However, it was the nodal experience of his father bailing him out of jail that pointed him in a new direction.

Nodal Experience Types

David and Ricky's nodal experiences interrupted their lives and pointed them in new directions. David's immersions in European travel and summer camp expanded his horizons and reoriented him in the world. Ricky's self-inflicted sufferings created turbulent family life. His experience in jail helped him grow up and demonstrated the nature of unconditional love. In both instances, David and Ricky became different men. Whereas David's immersions were planned, the fruit of those experiences was not what he expected. Ricky's self-inflicted sufferings, while not positive at the time, helped him grow up.

Figure 2 below identifies the five types of nodal experiences that surfaced. In addition, the table shows sub-categories of the five types. We have also supplied the number of responses identified in each type. The number of responses exceeds the number of those interviewed in this study because the respondents often reported more than one nodal experience.

Type	Responses
Immersions	
Camps/retreats	19
Events	8
Mission Trips	6
Group Gatherings	9
Travel	6
Total	48

Sufferings

Experiences		24
Awakenings		3
Reconciliations		2
	Total	29

Family Events

Birth of a child		9
Getting Married		4
Parenting		2
Moving		2
	Total	17

Competencies

Opportunity to lead		12
Rites of Passage events		2
	Total	14

Mentoring

	Total	7
	Overall Total	**115**

Figure 2

Immersions: Events, mission trips, and group gatherings

Nine young men reported that they had a nodal experience through an event. Dwight cited the birth of his first child. Recognizing this as a turning point in his life, the event that became nodal for him was his and his newborn son's baptisms on the same day. "Taking communion that day and being baptized with him was a moment of a new beginning for me."

Terry reports that his high school graduation was powerful. "I was proud of my accomplishment. I was not looking forward to going to high school, but did well enough anyway." In addition, Terry remarked, "First communion was a particularly spiritual moment. I felt different and very spiritual at that moment. It was like I was truly accepted by God." Although he was only ten at the time, that sticks with him. In both Dwight and Terry's cases, they were immersed in a Christian community that nurtured the nodal event that would impact them deeply.

Mission trips can create nodal experiences for young men. Twenty-year-old Jeff is waiting to join the marines. While in a holding pattern until his training begins, he exercises, spends time with friends, snowboards, and listens to music. His older brother, whom he respects, is a marine. Jeff's church's mission trips to Mexico were very meaningful to him. He likes to help others through manual labor. "It feels good to bring people from cardboard shacks to homes with sturdy walls and something other than a dirt floor." Coupled with this immersion, Jeff notes that a key experience in his life has been a college retreat weekend with his youth group. He likes the prayer, worship, and singing.

Mark's experience is similar to Jeff's. At twenty, Mark is in his second year of an architectural engineering program. He loves school, but his life is hectic. He drives in the country to relax. Mission trips have strongly influenced his life. "Going on so many mission trips made me aware of the blessings that I have living in this country, and I've become aware of the needs of other people. Mission trips build hope for life and create an interest in the welfare of other people."

Finally, our research shows significant group gatherings can become nodal experiences for young men. We were struck by the power of Alcoholics Anonymous and men's Bible studies and retreats. Aaron is a thirty-two-year-old steel worker who walked into the interview enormously confident. Ten minutes into the conversation, he wept as his life story unfolded. Aaron's father, whom he did not meet until he was five years old, was an alcoholic. His mother was divorced for a second time by the time Aaron was twelve. Feeling abandoned by his parents, he rebelled early. During his teens, he became addicted to alcohol and drugs and grew more violent. "I would get into fights four times a week," he said. At eighteen in a street fight, he threw a man through a plate glass window cutting him badly. When the man nearly bled to death, Aaron was frightened and asked God to help him with his anger.

Having used cocaine during his teenage years, Aaron turned to it again when work pressure overwhelmed him. The cocaine use put stress on his marriage. His lack of confidence led him to walk away from lucrative steel work because he couldn't handle the pressures of supervision. Thinking back he sees this as the turning point for him and his marriage.

A man from Aaron's church took him to an AA meeting. In this group, a spiritual counselor helped him center his life. Aaron was assigned an AA mentor who was a former biker and drug dealer. This less-than-subtle mentor "really got into my head," he says, and helped Aaron address his issues of abandonment and lack of self-confidence. After fourteen months of attending AA, Aaron is now the mentor of a recovering seventeen-year-old cocaine addict. In this young man, Aaron is essentially mentoring himself when he was a young and violent man.

Aaron talks now of the power of Kingdom Weekends offered by his church. These retreats are designed for adults to enter a spiritual journey through group Bible study and conversation, personal examination and devotion, and outdoor adventure. Having been a participant on a number of these weekends where he readily admits, "I cry all the time," he now has been trained to lead a Kingdom Weekend on behalf of his congregation.

There are so many significant moments in Aaron's story that it is difficult to identify them all. Certainly his suffering serves as backdrop and context for the unplanned and positive turn his life has taken. However, nodal experiences in the lives of young men gain additional power through their active reflection on the experience. In Aaron's case, it was significant that he had nearly killed someone. However, it didn't truly change his lifestyle, nor did he address his personal pain as a result. In fact, he gave up violence but kept the drugs. It was the group gatherings of AA and the Kingdom Weekends that created his nodal insights. If, indeed, his life-changing experience began with the shock of the fight, it wasn't until twelve years later that the nodal moment had its full effect through group gatherings that helped him discover and articulate his personal pain, need for healing, and power to go in a new direction.

Sufferings: Experiences, awakenings, and reconciliations

Our research also shows that suffering can create a powerful nodal moment for a young man.

Jerry works eighty hours a week. He grew up in what he calls a "perfect childhood." He said, "My family taught me right from wrong and the values I hold are derived from those childhood experiences." Jerry feels close to his father and has memories of doing "guy" things with him. "We have countless memories of working on cars together. We would do a lot of that. My dad loves cars and so we'd go out and work on cars." Jerry also reports that his grandparents played a large part in his upbringing. In fact, it was his grandparents who provided him with the most significant nodal experience of his life.

While he was growing up, his family often visited his grandparents' ranch. "I would get almost giddy with excitement going to the ranch. My grandfather was a very, very stern man, very tough, rugged. He was a rancher and always chewing tobacco. He was the stereotypical almost John Wayne-type of a rancher."

Jerry's grandmother suffered a debilitating stroke, so that his grandfather had to care for her. "When you watch two old people and the things that they have to do for each other and you see the love, that's got to be something in itself that molds you. When I saw the tender love and care—my grandmother also had Alzheimer's disease—Grandpa would take her food put it in a blender and he would blend it up, and that's what he fed my grandmother. To see this man—his calloused hands, just rough—just to see him put that spoon in her mouth and wipe her mouth and say, 'Okay, Ruby, I'm going to give you some water now' and lift that cup to her face. That's love, and even though it's not the greatest of situations, that's incredible."

Jerry's experience of observing the suffering of his grandparents and how they managed and responded deeply influenced him. Whether his grandfather knew he was teaching Jerry about dignity, love, and faithfulness we don't know. Nevertheless, those are the lessons Jerry learned.

We observed in Jerry and Aaron that immersions and sufferings are nodal experiences when they become redemptive. Aaron's story is of death and resurrection. Jerry's of love that became incarnate. Some nodal experiences provide bridges to the death and resurrection of Christ and the incarnate love of Jesus. We found that, for our young men, these nodal experiences served as parables and bridges to a God who immerses himself in human suffering.

Family events

The young men of our study are strongly impacted by the formation of their own families. Other research shows that forming a family domesticates young men, lowers their testosterone levels, and orients them toward others. It was not uncommon for a young man to tell us he ended his "wild child" phase when he got married and fathered a child.

Harvey is twenty-seven years old and his wife is a stay-at-home mom with their infant daughter. He comments that his wedding was, "the most significant moment in my life because everyone was at the same place at the same time. It was the ultimate." Harvey considers his wife his best friend.

Steve is eagerly awaiting the birth of his first child. In anticipation of the birth, he and his wife are considering returning to church. The birth of his child and the surrounding faith rituals are a point of re-engagement for him. "It's a big turning point," he says. Steve is looking for a church to provide what he had as a child. "Church is an important place for children in my opinion and in my family and in our tradition. I think it all comes back to what my family has done and what they've wanted for their children. As far back as the stories I hear, church was always there. I want to stick with what our family has done, not just because that's what they've done, but because it's made a difference, I think, for all of us." The anticipated birth of his child is a nodal moment for Steve. He is using this moment to reconnect with his family traditions. Family nodal experiences for these young men are times to pause and reflect on their upbringings. They either celebrate them, such as Steve, or they decide to "never do that to my family" and create new traditions and family practices.

What struck us in this research regarding marriage and family was how these young couples struggle to find a circle of friends. Unless they are living close to their immediate families, many of them described searching for a "home" or a place where they can find mutual support. These young couples are still emerging adults and recognize there is much to learn. In many cases, these young married men are still settling their core values and belief system. Marriage or the birth of a child is a reminder that there is work to be done sorting out who they are, what they stand for, and what they want to pass on to their children.

Moving is the final sub-category of family nodal experiences. These young men are mobile. Tony was born and raised in New York in a strong Italian family. To the shock and dismay of his family, especially his grandmother, he left for California to become a chef. When in California, Tony met a young woman with whom he is now engaged. He has moved into her family's home. Tony commented that the move to California was significant to him. No one in his family had ever done this before. He is still spinning from this experience trying to grasp the meaning of it all.

Competencies: Opportunities to lead and rites of passage

We heard from a number of those young men about the importance of earning their Eagle Scout badge. Although this achievement took place in their mid- to late teens, they were still basking in the glow of this achievement years later. A few noted that the rite of confirmation was a significant accomplishment and nodal experience for them. More often however, these young men spoke with pride of their own emerging leadership. Chris commented that it was spiritually significant to be a confirmation mentor and to chaperon a group of confirmation youth. David not only became an Eagle Scout but talks of how important it is to him to continue this work helping at the local food bank. Jud, an Eagle Scout, became a summer camp counselor in his late teens and early twenties. Likewise, Michael has been a counselor at his Presbyterian church camp.

In finding opportunities to lead, these young men recognize their emerging powers. Their identity is forming and they are claiming their own voice and gifts. The nodal moments provided in scouting or a three month summer of service at a camp or having their leadership affirmed has an impact upon them. Nic commented, "The pastor publicly described me as one of the brightest personalities in the youth."

Our instincts tell us that one of the keys to young men's ministry can be summarized in four words, "Give them meaningful work." We heard enough from these young men to recognize that they want to make a contribution to their community. We also heard that they are not often shown or given the opportunity to make such a contribution through the church.

Mentoring

We have written earlier about the role of fathers, grandfathers, older siblings, and extended family in shaping these young men. We want to affirm that mentoring relationships provide powerful nodal experiences for many in this study.

Ken told us his story of going to lunch with his boss. "There's been events in my life where I felt like God was just guiding me, like taking the job I did right out of college and being in a professional environment where the president of the firm took me out to lunch. He'd go, 'Geez, I don't want to talk about work, how are you with God?' It's pretty amazing to get into a work situation where you have somebody like that who's really not only mentoring you professionally, but is almost like a father figure and is concerned about your well-being, and not just your financial well-being, not just your family well-being, not just your professional well-being, but your spiritual well-being. He's a pretty amazing guy."

Ernie had a similar nodal experience. "I went to work for a food distributor and my boss there was very influential on me from a religious standpoint because he was a very devout Christian and was fairly forthright with his beliefs and welcoming as far as inviting me to different things that his church had going on to kind of incorporate that in my life."

Theological and Theoretical Considerations

God's Spirit is alive outside institutional religious practices. Nodal experiences occur in the most unlikely of locations and come from the most surprising sources. They occur at camps, in the words of bikers and bosses, are seen in the tender moments of care by a rough rancher, through the miracle of birth, and in new life, amid the shipwreck of addiction and violence.

God is loose in the world. The nodal experiences of these young men confirm how broadly God will reach to help young men become what God intends them to be. Jesus spoke of this when he described the Spirit to Nicodemus: "The wind blows where it chooses, and you hear the sound of it, but you do not know where it comes from or where it goes. So it is with everyone who is born of the Spirit" (John 3:8).

Singer and song writer Peter Mayer captured God's surprising and expansive presence in human affairs in song and poetry:

Hey, Hey, Hey, Hey
God is loose, God is loose

Hey, hey, God is loose in the world!
We got our maps and clues
Still we can't find the Spirit's nest
We hunt for miles and all the while
It paints the scenery,
Scatters in worlds and never rests.[2]

The lives of these young men demonstrate that God works through a broad spectrum of nodal experiences to surprise, inform, shape, redirect, and inspire. The question is, why does God choose such varied and mundane means to get "on the screens" of young men?

Psychologist James Marcia helps us understand the vital role nodal experiences play in young human development. Building on the work of Erik Eriksson, Marcia's theory of identity formation posits that in early adolescence young humans (male or female) fall into two categories; they are either identity-diffused or identity-foreclosed people.[3]

Identity-diffused adolescents have few strong commitments. In the words of *Mad Magazine,* they are the Alfred E. Newmans of the world who say, "What, me worry?"

Identity-foreclosed adolescents, on the other hand, have clear commitments that are mostly internalized messages from parents and their culture. They have not chosen, and generally do not consider, alternatives. Their motto might well be, "I know what I think, so don't confuse me with the facts."

As young men develop, they travel three roads psychologically. First, they can remain "identity-diffused" into their twenties. An expression of this type of young man is a "mook" found in the worlds of MTV and marketing. A mook is what you see on *The Man Show.* He is like a frat boy who sees women only as objects of desire and loves to party. Every spring mooks descend upon the beaches of Florida for Spring break. In our research, we have called the mook the "wild child" phase of young men. The self-identity of a mook remains essentially unformed. He has not gotten serious, or life has not challenged him to explore who he is. He is self-oriented but not self-insightful.

Another kind of identity-diffused person is a young man who has been so wounded or abandoned that he is lost. We see this clearly in Aaron, the steel worker. At age thirty-two, Aaron is just now beginning to discover who he is. His path to self-identity was frozen in anger and drug addiction. Aaron's "mookness" was a cover for his deep, personal anguish and pain.

The second psychological road a young man can take is to remain "identity-foreclosed." Unlike the mook, this young man is rigid and fixed in his identity. He has inherited his sense of self and is not particularly reflective. The extreme version of this phenomenon would be a young man who is a neo-Nazi, a reactionary, or fundamentalist. He does not have the ability, or is unwilling, to reflect on the world through the eyes and perspective of others. In fact, he feels threatened by other worldviews and perspectives.

More typical expressions of the identity-foreclosed young male can be seen in many college freshman, or new recruits in the military. These young men simply have not been challenged so their initial exposure to other worlds is unsettling. If they have been rooted well as children and are bonded with others, their foray out of their foreclosed world can be a time of discovery and wonder. We heard this in the young men who got involved in summer camps, mission trips, or other immersions that broadened their horizons.

The third path a young man can take in identity formation is what James Marcia called "identity-achieved."[4] The key to developing an "achieved identity" is an active search for commitment. The content of the commitment is not the only issue. What is critical is that commitments are made as the result of identity reflection, "in the course of which various possibilities have been seriously considered."[5] A young man forms his adult identity through an active search for his core commitments.

We heard this active search taking place throughout our research. What often triggered the search in sixty-three of eighty-eight of those interviewed was a nodal experience. The nodal experience pushed, disrupted, or invited the young man to explore his commitments. Marcia calls this experience moratorium.[6] During a time of moratorium, the identity of these young men is in limbo. They can no longer reside in the oblivious delusion or pain of identity-diffusion, nor can they be satisfied with the prior answers of identity-foreclosure.

Famed anthropologist, Arnold Van Gennep, called this event "liminality." The best way to understand liminality is to imagine standing in a doorway. In the room behind is the world you have always known. You may or may not have liked that room, but it is who you are (identity-diffused or identity-foreclosed). Having lived there most of your life, you are suddenly thrust toward the exit. You may or may not have chosen to go in this direction but it is now inevitable: you are moving toward the threshold. Standing in this doorway represents a nodal moment. Before you is a new room similar in some ways but very different in others. It is the life you are moving into. Unlike the room behind you, it is not clear as to what this room holds. In order for you to move into that new room you have to make decisions. How will you travel? Who or what will you take with you? What will you use as your guide? What do you want to come of this journey? What do you want to avoid? These questions surface because you are in the process of formulating your own identity as a young man.

Nearly all the young males interviewed who had a nodal experience described this phenomenon of identity-moratorium or liminality. Some were surprised to be thrust into the doorway; others grudgingly acknowledged they had to go there; still others could hardly wait and made intentional efforts to find and embrace the experience. Steel worker Aaron lived in the doorway for twelve years, insecure in the room behind him and afraid of the room in front of him. Ricky literally stood in the doorway of a jail long enough for his father to walk with him to a different life. David, the traveler and camp counselor, went through the doorway many times and found even more rooms to explore each time. In each case however, a nodal experience helped them form a new identity, often claiming a deeper faith and church life in the process.

Two of Jesus' followers were walking on the road to Emmaus following his crucifixion (Luke 24:13-35). They were having a sufferings nodal experience. Cleopas is discouraged by what has happened in Jerusalem. He tells the stranger walking with them, "But, we had hoped that he was the one to redeem Israel. Yes, and besides all this, it is now the third day since these things took place" (vs. 21). Cleopas' expectations have been shattered. "Our chief priests and leaders handed him over to be condemned to death and crucified him" (v. 20).

Everything Cleopas had learned about the Jewish expectation of the coming Messiah (identity-foreclosed) has proven to be false. Therefore, he and his traveling companion are trying to make sense of it all (identity-moratorium). Although they don't recognize Jesus, they travel with him and Jesus provides a different understanding of the Christ as the one who suffers so as to enter into glory. Jesus continues to travel with them (nodal experience or immersion) and eventually has supper with them. When the bread is broken, they recognize this stranger and afterward remark, "Were not our hearts burning within us while he was talking to us on the road, while he was opening the scriptures to us?" (vs. 32). Immediately, they rise to tell others of what they have seen and experienced. Identity-achieved Cleopas and his friend run through the threshold into a new room in which they proclaim, "The Lord has risen indeed!" (vs. 34). The nodal experiences of sufferings and immersion literally change the identity of Cleopas and his friend. They are transformed by these events. We witnessed these dynamics from Luke's gospel in many of the lives of the young men we interviewed.

Perhaps the most significant nodal experience in the New Testament is the story of Saul (Paul) on the road to Damascus (Acts 9: 1-30). A zealot for the Jews, Saul persecuted Christians and witnessed the stoning of Stephen. His identity is well-anchored in his Jewish and Roman heritages. However, all that changed on the road to Damascus where he experienced the living Lord and lost his sight (sufferings-awakenings). Saul is taken to Damascus and left for blind (moratorium-liminality). A local Christian, Ananias, gets the dubious job of taking care of Saul in his blindness. Unconvinced that Saul won't kill him, Ananias balks at his assignment. Eventually, he does go to Saul and lays hands on him (nodal experience-mentoring) and cures him. In addition, he baptizes Saul in the name of Jesus and feeds him. These powerful nodal events have a dramatic impact on Saul, and his identity and behavior change. The old Saul is literally left in the previous room, and Paul walks through the threshold into the Greek world with the gospel of Jesus Christ.

Implications for the Church and Its Ministry

The types of nodal experiences identified in the research point to strategies for ministry:

- Create opportunities for immersions through retreats, mission trips, travel, regular group gatherings, and other events.

- Recommend young men in your congregation for work on outdoor ministry staffs. Encourage them to invest a summer in Christian leadership.

- Listen to and reflect together upon the stories of young men who have worked in outdoor ministry or are serving in the military.

- Help young men find employment.

- Recognize that the birth of a child is a nodal experience for young men; utilize this time to build relationships. Offer opportunities for them to connect more fully with other fathers and children's ministry.

- As a supervisor take young male employees under your wing. Get to know them and share the Good News with them.

- Create men's ministry study groups that meet regularly. Use the *Masterbuilder's Bible* offered by Lutheran Men in Mission to anchor these gatherings.

- Sponsor Kingdom Weekends (retreats) like those Aaron experienced.

- Provide space, hospitality, and relationships to AA groups and similar support networks.

- Be attentive to the sufferings of young men and seek opportunities to talk about that suffering.

- Reach out to, embrace, and claim the young men in your jails, treatment centers, and homeless shelters.

- Invite, invite, and invite young men into leadership such as mentoring a confirmation or leading in a mission trip.

- Recognize that newly married men, or new fathers, may be looking for a church. Identify them and provide hospitality, a cordial invitation, regular contact, and instruction.

- Create Bible study groups for those recently married.

Remember that nodal experiences often happen outside the walls of the church, so be looking for them. Remember, God is loose in the world!

chapter 6

CRISES, STRESS,

AND A BALANCED LIFE

"Men are like M&Ms—hard on the
outside and soft on the inside."
—Young male interviewee

Rock musicians are often ahead of researchers when it comes
to articulating what is taking place in the lives of the young.
Bob Dylan served this role in the 1960s; Eddie Vetter of Pearl
Jam, Kurt Cobain of Nirvana, and hip hop artist Tupac were the
prime "pop prophets" in the 1980s and 1990s. More recently,
the Christian band POD has spoken eloquently of what we
discovered regarding these young men. POD's song, "Youth
of the Nation," serves as an iconic anthem giving voice to the
crises in the lives of many young adults, most certainly males.
Released in 2001, the song quickly swept the charts filling the
airwaves with their pain and a cry for help.

Johnny boy always played the fool
He broke all the rules
So you would think he was cool
He was never really one of the guys
No matter how he tried

Often thought of suicide
It's kind of hard when you ain't got no friends
He put his life to an end
They might remember him then
You cross the line and there's no turning back
Told the world how he felt
With the sound of a gat.

Who's to blame for the lives that tragedy claims
No matter what you say
It don't take away the pain
That I feel inside, I'm tired of all the lies
Don't nobody know why
It's the blind leading the blind
I guess that's the way the story goes
Will it ever make sense
Somebody's got to know
There's got to be more to life than this
There's got to be more to everything I thought exists.
    —"Youth of the Nation" POD, *Satellite,* 2001

    Young men are often living in crisis. Nearly all the young men we interviewed spoke of crises in their lives. In fact, seventy of eighty-eight interviewees reported having experienced or been strongly impacted by a personal crisis.

    There is a great variety of trauma in their lives; their crises include divorce, alcoholism, crime, mental problems, jail, car accidents, financial calamity, job loss, suicide, multiple unresolved family issues, and the death of friends, family, or loved ones. As Christians who know of the persuasiveness of evil, we shouldn't be surprised by the volume of ways that "life's train goes off the rails" but we were struck by the significant role that crisis plays in the lives of these young men. As POD's song states, "I guess that's the way the story goes."

Whereas crisis events serve as an important backdrop or context for many of the young men we interviewed, the way they respond to these crises is equally significant. When they arrive at a significant point of pain, distress, or fear, they are often forced to ask the question POD raises: "There's got to be more to life than this/There's got to be more to everything I thought exists." When this question is engaged by a young man living in the context of a trusted relationship with a caring, meaningful ministry, transformation often occurs.

Max

At thirty-one, Max is engaged and living with his fiancée on the East Coast. He is a carpenter. Although raised in the church and currently an active member, it has not insulated him from calamity. Like so many interviewed, Max's life was deeply influenced by his parents' divorce when he was a young boy. For years, he thought he had caused the divorce. His self recrimination became a dominant internal voice and fostered a sense of guilt and personal inadequacy. In his case, divorce impoverished his family. "We grew up dirt poor and I felt that I was less than other children in the class," he commented. "Kids came to school with nice clothes and my tennis shoes had holes in them." Max notes that there were times when he was on the streets living hand-to-mouth, without friends and with little family contact. His bitterness stays with him as he still does not talk to his father and one of his brothers. His brother has excluded him and everyone else in the immediate family.

In spite of support from an uncle and a Big Brother mentor who "spoke about God and the church a lot," by the age of sixteen, Max had not bonded with any positive male role model, yet he thought he knew everything. As he looks back, he realizes, "I didn't know I didn't know." Reflecting on the teachings of his Big Brother he says, "I couldn't hear any of that." Max became an alcoholic and street drug addict.

At his lowest moment Max decided to enter treatment, encouraged by a man in the church who Max says, "Just understood me and my situation." In addition, at this point a remnant of his family supported him. This was a powerful transition for Max. He has been clean for three years and is now active in his congregation.

His low self regard still lurks, however. Recently engaged, Max comments that "I never thought that anyone would want to spend their life with me." When he and his girlfriend decided on a wedding ring and it dawned on him that he was officially engaged, he marveled that someone would care for him.

Max continues to struggle with finances and his feelings. He has difficulty expressing his anger, hurt, sorrow, and pain, as well as joy and happiness. His recovery program helps him get in touch with his feelings. He celebrates that he has a roof over his head, friends, family, and fiancée. Most significantly, God is back in his life and he enjoys hearing Scripture shared at recovery Bible studies. "I can see the light come in," he beams. Max prays in the morning and at night, at work and most anytime. He acknowledges that God guides his thinking and gives him "I.B.M.s," that is, "itsy-bitsy miracles."

Billy

Like Max, Billy is profoundly shaped and scarred by his parents' divorce. His interview was one of the most moving. At age twenty, Billy attends a community college on the West

Coast and is studying to be a nurse. He works as a day-care provider for kindergarten through sixth graders. He shares an apartment with two friends, choosing to live on his own because of conflicts at home. He and his family have been active in the church his entire life.

Billy has lived "everywhere" because his father served in the military. Seven years ago, his mother had an affair with another man and left the family. This experience provides a central focus of Billy's life. He reports feeling "broken inside" and betrayed. "I'm on a quest for wholeness," he laments.

His quest has led him into many unhealthy relationships. He reports getting involved with other people very quickly, especially with girlfriends. One need not be a psychoanalyst to see that Billy is seeking attachment trying to repair the torn bond with his mother. His most recent relationship with a girlfriend ended because God and religion were not part of her life. Her parents had divorced four times and he was worried that she would follow the same pattern.

Billy and the rest of his family returned to the West Coast after his mother left. He says it has been a "bummer" because his friends' parents were divorcing, too. "It all smells the same," he comments sadly. It is interesting to note that he equates this pain with the sense of smell. The sense of smell is the most primal and primitive for humans. Billy's use of this sense in metaphorically describing his parents' divorce points to how primary his pain resides.

The church is critical life support for Billy. "Church is where I get my power, re-energize my battery, relax, and get comfortable. I'm glad in church and think about life when I'm in church." In addition, an aunt and a football coach play large roles in his life. "Aunt Mona and Uncle Mike have great kids, and they have a whole new perspective on life." These people serve as a surrogate family for Billy.

Exploring Crises

In 1997 the rock band Everclear wrote what some claim was the anthem for the decade titled "Father of Mine." Once again the words of the rock poets speak clearly of the crises of young men.

Father of mine
tell me where have you been
you know I just closed my eyes
my whole world disappeared
father of mine
take me back to the day
when i was still your golden boy
back before you went away
i remember blue skies
walking the block
i loved it when you held me high
i loved to hear you talk
you would take me to the movie
you would take me to the beach
you would take me to a place inside
that is so hard to reach
Father of mine
tell me where did you go
you had the world inside your hand
but you did not seem to know
father of mine
tell me what do you see
when you look back at your wasted life
and you don't see me
i was ten years old
doing all that i could
it wasn't easy for me
to be a scared white boy
in a black neighborhood
sometimes you would send me a birthday card

with a five dollar bill
i never understood you then
and i guess i never will

Chorus:
daddy gave me a name
my dad he gave me a name
then he walked away
daddy gave me a name
then he walked away
my dad he gave me a name
father of mine
tell me where have you been
i just closed my eyes
and the world disappeared
father of mine
tell me how do you sleep
with the children you abandoned
and the wife i saw you beat
i will never be safe
i will never be sane
i will always be weird inside
i will always be lame
now I'm a grown man
with a child of my own
and i swear that I'm not going to let her know
all the pain i have known
   —"Father of Mine," Everclear, *So Much for the
      Afterglow,* 1997

What is significant to note is the lack of capitalization regarding the personal pronoun "I." It is as if Everclear has captured the sense of insignificance that both Max and Billy feel as a result of their family experiences. The only variation in the pattern of this song comes when the singer speaks of the kind of parent he intends to be for his child. At this point, the personal pronoun "I" is capitalized as if to defiantly say, "I'll make it different, I'll be different, and my parenting and family will be different."

We hear this struggle to move from "i" to "I" within the stories of Max and Billy. Significantly, their journeys through family and personal crises have incorporated a giving over of trust to God and the support of members of the body of Christ in their respective churches. We'll revisit these themes later in this chapter when we discuss effective outreach methods to young adult males in crisis.

Divorce is not the only crisis identified in this study, but it is certainly one of the largest issues raised. In fact, family issues far exceed any other crisis mentioned in the study. One can hear the lament and struggle of family in songs such as "Jesus of Suburbia" by Green Day. The song speaks of the pain of living in a world where children can feel abandoned by parents consumed by their own needs and left to fend for themselves on a "steady diet of soda pop, Ritalin, and television."

While all generations of children have experienced absentee or abusive parents, the song points to what seems to be a growing problem in family life, namely that many adults in these young men's lives are behaving less than responsibly. These adults are in crisis, and their children feel neglected. Rising divorce rates and the revolving door of live-in boyfriends rather than real fathers can play havoc with the lives of young men. Just at a time when they most need a stable role model, supportive love, and caring direction, they experience just the opposite. It's no wonder that family crises led the list of crises in our survey.

In his book, *Counseling Men,* Philip Culbertson says this about family:

No human being has avoided being shaped by a family context at the deepest levels of identity. All families are intensely emotional systems, even those whose interaction exhibits no overt emotion. Our families shape our values and assumptions for us, before we are old enough to make up our own minds. Because these families are the only context we know intimately for the first several years of our lives, we quickly come to assume that what we see in our own families is "normal," the way things ought to be in every family. (Minneapolis: Fortress Press, 1994, p. 49)

When young men experience a "norm" in family life that is short on values or emotionally damaging, they can often struggle with being good fathers or husbands. We saw evidence of that struggle in our interviews.

In chapter 5, "Life-Defining Experiences," we explored crises from the perspective of nodal experiences. The distinction to be made between the crises referenced there and the crises focused on here is that not all crises lead to nodal experiences. Not all crises have positive, transformative impacts on the lives of young men.

The following table identifies the range of issues that surfaced. The number of responses exceeds the total number of those interviewed because some respondents were experiencing more than one crisis.

Type of Crisis	Number of Responses	Total
Family Issues		109
Parents' divorce	36	
Crisis in family dynamics	15	
Personal divorce	11	
Sibling divorce	9	
Internal Personal Crises		24
Relational problems/ inability to connect	7	
Mental health issues	6	
Health issues	4	
Assorted personal issues	4	
Suicide	2	
College decisions	1	

Type of Crisis	Number of Responses	Total
External Personal (Behavioral) Crises		23
Alcohol and drug abuse	14	
Teen or young adult misbehavior	9	
Time Management/Job/Finance Crises		21
Death Crises		10
Parent	5	
Friend	3	
Own child	2	
Miscellaneous Crises		9
Victim of crime	4	
Accidents	4	
Witness protection	1	
Total Crises		114

Table 2

Family Issues

In Max and Billy, we have referenced the profound impact of divorce on these young men. Certainly, not all divorces create such trauma and in some situations divorces change families for the better. In the cases of the majority of those we interviewed whose parents divorced, the effect upon these young men was traumatic and in many cases long lasting.

While often romanticized and idealized, families present mixed emotions and experiences for young men. Families serve as the primary care, nurture, and socialization unit for all human beings, at least initially. Reformer Martin Luther thought of families as the primary foundation of all civilization. Families have great power to shape and influence us.

For young adult males, families are never neutral. They have impact, sometimes creating crises.

Raising their own family translates into an ongoing crisis for many of the young men we interviewed. Jerome's family crisis centers on his inability to manage his impatience. Jerome is a salesman, the father of three children. "With three children, I'm on the run most days chasing after them and going through their activities and being a big part of their lives." As a result, Jerome wrestles with achieving balance in his life and having time "just for me and just for my wife and me." Jerome reports that "listening to them [children] laugh and giggle and have fun, you just can't beat that," but he says his biggest concern is being a parent. "My biggest struggle is to be a patient father. I know I need to do a better job at it, but it's a constant struggle to try and be more patient to both my wife and my kids."

Establishing a new family while maintaining old family ties also creates crises for some of these young men. At age thirty-two, Clark's family lives in crisis. Clark grew up in a close-knit farm family in Minnesota. He grew up as the "good son," the oldest of three. He was and remains the responsible child in the family. In his family of origin, he rarely experienced any conflict. All of that changed after college when Clark got married. He moved back to the farm and tensions escalated between his wife and mother to such an extent that he and his wife left the farm. Clark now has little contact with his family of origin. His close relationship with his younger brother is shattered, and he and his wife are ostracized from his extended, biological family.

Creating new families by blending prior families can also cause crisis. Twenty-year-old Del grudgingly lives at home with his parents while he attends community college. When Del was in fifth grade his mother died of cancer. His maternal grandmother blamed Del's father for his mother's death, accusing him of not paying enough attention to the complications of her condition. The bitterness runs so deep that when his grandfather died, his grandmother never told the rest of the family of her husband's death. She didn't want them at the funeral. A year after Del's mother died, his father remarried. Del has never liked his stepmother, his three stepsisters, and one stepbrother. Del's family attended church regularly until his mother died. When his father remarried, one stepsister put up "a big fuss" about going to church, so the family quit attending. Del has resentment toward his stepfamily and has decided to call the family housekeeper, "Mom." The tragic death of Del's mother and the shockwaves in the aftermath continue to roil Del's family.

Some of the crises these young men experience in their families have to do with their own lack of maturity. At thirty-three years old, Tony is a successful salesman. Tony's parents divorced when he was two, remarried each other, and then divorced a second time when he was ten. "It was a bad experience," he wryly comments. Tony grew up in the church, left after confirmation, and has now gotten involved again. Tony is struggling with his own marriage. This struggle centers on his desire to return to his earlier life as a golf pro. He readily acknowledges that he has been selfish in this regard. In his current job he travels three nights a week leaving his wife and two daughters alone at home. Tony's selfishness is manifested and compounded by his alcoholism. At the age of fifteen, he was ordered by the court to attend AA meetings and has been in and out of recovery since then. Tony admits his crises are caused by his selfishness.

Twenty-four-year-old Arnold grew up in a dysfunctional family. Arnold was abused as a child; his mother beat him twice a week with spoons, spatulas, and belts. After the beatings, he was expected to lie in bed on his bruises. She nearly strangled him on more than one occasion. His father was abusive as well; fortunately he was not often home. His parents eventually divorced and Arnold was raised by his mother. His family moved every year of his life through his sixteenth birthday. Arnold is a high school drop-out living on disability. He damaged his back in a severe car accident. Arnold is being treated for bipolar disorder and has attempted suicide. Arnold was married and has one son. He and his wife divorced after Arnold had an affair and a daughter was born from this extra-marital relationship. Arnold and his former wife are now looking to remarry. In the meantime, he is in a custody battle with his mother over his daughter. "She just wants another child to beat," he says. The girl's mother, his former wife, is a drug addict.

While difficult to imagine, Arnold's story of family dysfunction carries an element of hope. Arnold was adopted by his church's men's group, led by David, a caring committed men's ministry leader. After meeting Arnold through his aunt, David invited Arnold to Bible studies and took him on a men's snow retreat called a Kingdom Weekend. "We had a huge snowball fight on the retreat," comments Arnold. These activities and this relationship have had a huge impact on Arnold. He has made a commitment to "prove to others that I'm not crazy." In reflecting upon his previous suicide attempts, Arnold says, "I didn't die when I did; I didn't succeed." Arnold confesses, "I gave my bipolar to God."

It is difficult to know what will happen for Arnold. There is much discouragement, yet Arnold has met a caring group of older men, and one male mentor in particular. It is this ministry that is currently making the difference. We heard this theme over and over again as we discussed crises with these young men. If there was to be a change, if there was to be improvement in their situations, it often took place through the caring guidance of another man or men helping them heal, grow up, refocus, recover, and rebuild.

Internal personal crises

Young men struggle with internal personal crises: loneliness, mental illness, physical health problems, and vocational decisions. We were struck by how often these young men spoke of loneliness due to a lack of connection, especially with peers. Whether it was a new college student moving out of the home for the first time or the professional worker or businessman well established in a career and raising a family, we often heard them speak of isolation and a yearning for relationships.

Many of these young men long for others of similar interests and life situations. Phil, age twenty-seven, is not a loner or without people in his life. He is happily married and enjoys his one-year-old daughter. He considers his wife his best friend. Phil has two buddies with whom he enjoys racing slot cars. At first glance, some might question why Phil is having problems with relationships. Phil and his wife struggle because they can't find other couples like themselves who are young and Christian. They are desperately looking for community and are even considering moving in order to find it.

Like Phil, Wallace is married to "the love of his life" and enjoying his children. Wallace works in a highly professional field that he finds gratifying. Yet Wallace expresses great frustration in not having close, day-to-day relationships with other people his age who share similar interests.

Another relational crisis identified, especially by the younger of these men, emerges out of relationships with women. Dan attends a liberal arts college and considers himself a "usually happy-go-lucky people person." Yet, he struggles with his ex-girlfriend. He's not exactly sure what happened; the relationship still confounds him.

Reggie is well established in a career in criminal justice. He values highly the role fathers play in the lives of their children and would like to be a father. Reggie struggles with managing his money and would like "to find a wife." The search is not going well.

Twenty-year-old Jack loves golf and hockey. His life is stressful. "It's always the girl thing," he notes. "I'm just trying to figure it out." Jack suffers from Attention Deficit Disorder and struggles with making friends.

One could dismiss these crises as simply matters of dating and growing up, but there is more to them. These young men identified these issues as serious, intense, and often painful for them.

Along with relational issues, mental health crises are significant to many of these young men. Young men are twice as likely to be physically abused as females. For every young female suffering from an emotional disorder there are four males with emotional difficulties. Five out of six males suffer from Attention Deficit Hyperactive Disorder, a debilitating mental health problem that creates many male behavioral problems. These examples are not shared to minimize the mental health issues in women; they simply illustrate that mental health problems are significant in young men and lead to societal and social difficulties.

Some of these young men struggle with depression, often in silence. Bryce lives in the "macho culture" of the Hill Country of Texas. After graduating from college with a degree in pharmacy, Bryce was uncertain about his future: "I struggled with the direction my life was going and lived in a relatively numb emotional state." Finally, Bryce realized his illness and went to see a doctor who treated his depression.

Marty is a twenty-eight-year-old college student with a genetic predisposition to anxiety-depression disorder. His anxiety prevents him from driving. His illness is a form of obsessive-compulsiveness. Marty is now on medication for his illness, yet it remains a concern for him. Unlike Bryce, a significant part of Marty's treatment is his faith and life in the church. "The church has become a surrogate home for me," he notes. Many of these internal crises are interrelated and caused by abuse or the fractured relationships in our atomized society. We have discovered that when the church (often in the form of older men) meets these young men in their immediate pain or struggle significant ministry takes place that is well received and healing.

External personal (behavioral) crises

It is no secret to law enforcement or car insurance companies that young men often wreak havoc on themselves and others. Our data shows that most of their destructive behaviors are self generated or self inflicted. Ninety percent of all discipline problems in our schools are caused by young males. Fully 85 percent of all non-violent criminals in prison are males and 90 percent of all violent criminals are males. In addition, young men are fifteen times more likely to be victims of crime than are women. In other words, men abuse one another. There are many explanations offered for this behavior, including upbringing, lack of jobs, poor vocational options, poverty, racial discrimination, and so forth. The cause is complex, but it is important to add testosterone to this list. Young men have ten times the testosterone of females. Testosterone is the hormone of human aggression. It gives men beards, big muscles, and a more aggressive attitude, so much so that in a cultural study of 122 countries, men made the weapons in 121 of them.[1] When there is to be a war it is most likely started and mostly fought by men.

Our study shows that twenty-one of the young men interviewed had experienced some kind of self-generated crisis either as misbehaving teens or, more significantly, through the use and abuse of drugs and alcohol.

Jessie is a classic illustration of violent behavior connected to substance abuse. Although only twenty, Jessie has repeatedly been in trouble with the law. He has spent significant time in juvenile detention centers and jails. He links his difficulties to his drinking. Jessie appears to have inherited his susceptibility to alcohol—his father is an alcoholic, as was his grandfather. His father had been in recovery for twenty-four years and his grandfather started an AA group. Jessie's recovery began when Mark, a plumber, visited him in a detention center. Mark talked to him about God and gave him a Bible. Jessie says that Mark was central to his recovery and conversion.

Eli is an alcoholic. At twenty-three, he has already been in a serious car accident caused by his drinking. It scared him, and for awhile he bargained with God about quitting drugs and alcohol if he lived through the injuries of the accident. This promise lasted a short time. He began to drink again. Eli says he is concerned with having a "saved soul and a wasted life." He says he needs to "get my act together, finish my education, and not be doing minimal work." As is often the case with addiction, Eli is incapable or unwilling to recover. He sees himself as a dreamer letting his life slip away. There are presently no significant male figures in Eli's life.

Roger speaks of a "raging alcoholic period" in his life occasioned by his divorce and the death of his father. Roger loved his father deeply and stayed angry with God over his father's death for a long time. Roger is a "tough guy" who enjoys ranching, physical labor, and horseback riding. Roger gave us the metaphor for many men in this chapter. He said, "Men are like M&Ms, hard on the outside and soft on the inside." This describes Roger.

Like the prodigal son, Roger initiated his recovery by himself. He walked into his kitchen in May of 2003 and said, "What am I doing?" This was the beginning of a new spiritual journey for him. What now sustains his recovery is participation in two churches. Initially, he attended a large, nondenominational church where an older couple introduced themselves to him and befriended him. "It was an answer to prayer. They stayed in touch and helped me discover that I believed in God and was just mad at him." Later, Roger returned to his own congregation in his small town in Texas where he says it "feels good to be back home." Following the interview, Roger hugged another rancher friend in the congregation and exchanged an "I love you." Their sincere mutual expression of affection based upon friendship and their shared faith struck us as genuine and healthy but rare in Roger's subculture. The young men we interviewed spoke often of the need for cultural and congregational permission to be affectionate and supportive of one another.

Time management, jobs, and financial crises

Navigating today's complex economic and cultural world is a challenge for our young men. We have clustered a variety of issues relating to these complexities and challenges: time management, career, and financial concerns. As young men enter the mainstream of American society, finding a job and supporting oneself and one's dependents can be a major struggle. Nearly a quarter of those we interviewed spoke of these matters as a crisis. Other comments relating to work and financial demands indicate nearly all our respondents are thinking about these issues. For young men, finding a meaningful and sustaining career figures into discovering purpose and vocation as well as a livelihood.

Paul, thirty-one, is a carpenter earning an average income. He is married and has a three-year-old daughter. He works six to seven days a week and says he spends most of his income paying bills. He is struggling to find time to build a home for his family so that they can move out of their RV and make room for the new baby coming.

Rudy is thirty-four years old, single, and a steel worker with a good income. He describes his adolescence and young adult life as his "wild child" years. Rudy is now at a crossroads and the stress shows in his face. He has been invited into management in which he will supervise several workers and the responsibility weighs on him heavily. He notes that his body is breaking down. He is constantly physically stressed. His organizational skills are taxed. His job is making him crazy and he's considering more schooling.

Albert is twenty-three years old and works as an inventory manager. He lives at home with his parents and hopes to move out and attend college but he doesn't know what to study. He concludes that he made a bad choice waiting to go to college and feels stuck. "I was hovering and now I'm moving on."

Twenty-two-year-old Bernie is a paradox. When he entered the room for the interview, he came across as awkward and introverted. He had a clean cut, sort of a "Happy Days" Richie Cunningham look to him. That was an illusion. Bernie is a former punk rock band member, a mobile hip hop DJ, plays guitar, bass, and drums. He loves paintball, which he finds "very invigorating because it's done outside with lots of running." He also likes bonsai tree gardening, noting that it builds patience. He used drugs in high school and was a contrarian. He was home schooled because of his disruptive behavior. Bernie works forty to sixty hours per week at a bio-tech company. His hectic life is at a crossroads. He is looking for a career, and senses he has many choices. He is intelligent and resourceful, yet he has not found his place or purpose.

Paul, Rudy, Albert, and Bernie provide a cross section of the young men struggling with financial responsibilities, living on low or medium wages, and overwhelmed by the demands of jobs they don't particularly care about. All four of these young men have been active in a congregation but are not currently active or are only marginally involved now. While struggling with the big issues of identity, purpose, and economic viability, they do not see the church as a place for support, guidance, or discernment. We noted earlier the vital contribution a caring, older man can provide with a young man weathering such a crisis. Congregations that wish to engage young men can also be communities that help them sort out their sense of vocation, and might well provide vocational and employment guidance. Tending the spirituality of young men might well be accessed through exploration of vocation and career.

Tim's story is illustrative of this possibility. At thirty-four years old, Tim is a divorced former marine who fought in Operation Desert Storm. He is a giant of a man who is training to become a police officer. His marine experience was the most significant time in Tim's life. He says, "The marines were a source of great pride and influence for me and I still see the world through the eyes of a marine living by the code, 'God, country, family.'" He left the military after six years thinking it would save his marriage; it did not. When he left the marines, he became manager of a hardware supply store that paid well, but he despised the work.

Tim looks up to his older brother who is an active Christian. Tim longs for a life like that of his older brother—a wife, family, and meaningful job. His older brother has drawn Tim into a congregation. His brother is building on Tim's conversion to Christianity while on guard duty in the marines.

Tim feels alive when he attends church with his brother's family. He prays his marine prayer every day. This Christian family and congregation have communicated to Tim that "they understand what I'm going through." They recognize his vocational crisis and are walking with him, encouraging, and supporting him as he moves into a new life as a police officer. Tim has discovered in his older brother and his new congregation something he did not experience in the church in which he grew up. He experienced that church to be "money hungry," the leaders indiscreet, and the rituals boring. Tim has experienced the church negatively and positively, responding now to the congregation that recognizes and embraces him in his marital brokenness and vocational struggles.

Death and circumstantial crises

A group of these young men experienced calamity for which there seemed to be no cause or explanation. In this regard, these young men are no different than the general population. Accidents, death, trauma, crime, and flukes of nature make up a big part of the human condition. The way the church responds to young men who are struggling with these issues can make a significant difference in their lives and faith.

Ricky's story serves as a model for ministry to young men experiencing such unexplainable crises. Ricky has been active in a church his entire life. At twenty-seven years old and married, he is employed as an art director in an advertising firm. His father is Mexican, his mother is white, and he has two older sisters. His father was a career officer in the air force, an active Roman Catholic. He was a generous and highly regarded man. He retired from the air force and soon after died of a heart attack at age forty-four. His death was a staggering blow to the family and to Ricky. Ricky reevaluated himself and acted and dressed differently, meaning more "adult-like."

The church helped Ricky's family manage their land and developed a scholarship fund so Ricky could attend college. He says the pastor was "like a grandfather to me." Upon returning from college, Ricky met a new pastor who greeted him with the words, "Wassup Dawg?" Ricky commented that "no pastor ever spoke his language before and he became hooked." In addition, he was invited to use his artistic abilities in worship, creating PowerPoint images relating to the worship themes. His new pastor put up pieces of newsprint around the church and asked Ricky to draw his spiritual images and reflections during the service. Ricky's drawings received great feedback from the members who stay after church to view and interpret the images. Ricky's images are not just "visual noise," but translated by the membership, they shed light on the gospel and create community.

Ricky's story highlights important ministry practices that are effective in relating to young men living in crises. Upon the death of his father, congregational members, especially an older man, stepped in and helped the family financially, spiritually, and vocationally. A new congregation and pastor built a bridge to Ricky and encouraged the use of his artistic gifts. As a result, Ricky has weathered a tragedy, gotten a good education, found a job that he enjoys, and identified a ministry that is valued by his congregation.

Three Ways to Understand Crises

Self-centeredness

In the book of Romans, the apostle Paul spends the first three chapters discussing the rebellious, sinful condition of humanity. In summary, he writes:

> There is no one who is righteous, not even one;
> there is no one who has understanding,
> there is no one who seeks God.
> All have turned aside, together they have become worthless;
> there is no one who shows kindness,
> there is not even one. . . .
> There is no fear of God before their eyes.
> —Romans 3:10-12, 18

Paul aptly describes the rebellious "wild child" character of some of our young men who fit the profile of self-destructive people wreaking havoc on themselves and those closest to them.

Inspired by Paul's writings, Martin Luther described sin using the Latin phrase *incurvatus in se,* which means "self turned in on self." Sin is life that is all about me, my needs, my interests, my pursuits, and my personal enjoyment and achievement. This self-centeredness does not make much room for God, others, and the larger world.

We have observed such self-centeredness in the crises of some young men in this study. When they put their golf careers ahead of their families, overindulge in drugs and alcohol, lash out in violence, squander college opportunities, or ignore their responsibilities to employers, friends, or families these young men are *incurvatus in se,* turned in upon themselves thus creating many of their crises.

Trapped in sin

Later in Romans, the apostle Paul identifies a second under-standing of the human condition and human crises: "I do not understand my own actions. For I do not do what I want, but I do the very thing I hate. . . . For I do not do the good I want, but the evil I do not want is what I do" (Romans 7:15, 19). Here Paul is describing the human con-dition not in terms of personal rebellion, but in terms of bondage. There is evil outside and within that takes charge of us. Luther called this the bondage of the will. Humans live in the illusion that they have free will and free choices and can choose correctly. While not denying that humans have a will, Luther argued that it is an enslaved will. What seemly appears to be an oxymoron is, in reality, a true description of our human condition. We can imagine living the perfect life, being the perfect husband, selecting the perfect job, or being the perfect parent, but we cannot do what we imagine. We are trapped in our inconsistencies, our own weaknesses and the power of evil. So, whereas these young men make choices, they make them in a trapped condition; they are imperfect beings unable to perform what they promise or generate what they imagine.

We see bondage in the stories shared in this chapter. Many of these young men imagine being drug free but remain addicted. They choose to go to college but their immaturity destroys the opportunity. They work hard on their marriages only to have them fail. They strive to control their tempers and be patient with themselves, their children, their spouses, and their coworkers only to lose control in moments of high stress. Their crises arise from their sinful nature as well as of their own bad choices. Their choices are made in the web of sin and evil, and the results are often calamitous.

Living in chaos

Finally, the apostle Paul describes human crises in terms of global and cosmic chaos. For these young men, crises are not just an expression of selfish rebellion or an enslaved will, they occur at the hands of a chaotic cosmos that sweeps them along.

> "For the creation waits with eager longing for the revealing of the children of God; for the creation was subjected to futility, not of its own will but by the will of the one who subjected it, in hope that the creation itself will be set free from its bondage to decay and will obtain the freedom of the glory of the children of God. We know that the whole creation has been groaning in labor pains until now; and not only the creation, but we ourselves" (Romans 8:19-23a).

In this passage, Paul describes human crises in terms of the whole creation's brokenness or dysfunction. It is as if an avalanche is triggered and sweeps down a mountain; no matter who started the slide, those standing below are bound to be hurt or swept away.

Our young men often identified their crises in these chaotic terms. One young man's mother died at an early age, another struggles with a life-threatening illness, yet another is victimized and abused by his parents. Others suffer from depression, mental illness, and trauma—none of it of their own making. Their crises come out of the "groaning creation" with no understandable sense of fairness or causation.

Theological and Theoretical Considerations

We have cited how important it is for young men going through a crisis to have older male mentors, or congregational support to guide them in times of crises. Christian family members or congregations can intervene on their behalf. If these young men are living destructively, an intervention can take the form of tough love. When they fail to achieve their aspirations, an intervention can take the form of understanding and support as well as wise counsel during times of failure. When young men are victims of arbitrary calamities, this intervention can take the form of support (such as college tuition) or presence and empathy. We have seen in these stories that it is appropriate and necessary for those doing ministry with young men to intervene in times of crises.

Martin Luther described this role: "All who are called masters stand in the place of parents."[2] What Luther meant is that all adults are parents (i.e. interveners, guides, and empathizers) to the young. Luther fully expected that adults would act on behalf of the young in order that they may be guided and supported while growing up. Dietrich Bonhoeffer used the phrase, "pro me,"[3] to capture the same concept. When young men are in crisis they need someone who is "pro me" to be with them, most importantly older, responsible Christian males. The goal is to care for them and to help them understand that Christ is with them during times of crisis.

In Romans, the apostle Paul celebrates and proclaims this good news.

> *But now,* (emphasis ours) apart from law, the righteousness of God has been disclosed, and is attested by the law and the prophets, the righteousness of God through faith in Jesus Christ for all who believe. For there is no distinction, since all have sinned and fall short of the glory of God; they are now justified by his grace as a gift, through the redemption that is in Christ Jesus. (Romans 3:21-24)

Here Paul provides a theological description of the crises that encounter young people: rebellion, bondage, and chaos. Had Paul stopped at simply describing the human situation, his would be a depressing message. Paul, however, goes on to proclaim God's intervention in Jesus Christ. He does this by interrupting the accounts of calamity and crisis to say that God in Christ is intervening, changing, and redirecting the crises and calamities young men inflict or incur. This is the good news that in the midst of and beyond the immediate pain, alienation, and sheer "cussedness" of being a young man, Christ intervenes, claims them, redirects them, gives them hope beyond the immediate crisis, and promises them new life and purpose.

Implications for the Church and Its Ministry

Steve is a big man who speaks with a Carolina drawl. At thirty-three, he is a successful carpenter, but Steve is hurting. His ex-wife had several affairs which led to their divorce. Coming from a conservative and traditional family, he could not imagine that anyone would break a trusted marriage covenant. It has rocked Steve's world which places high value on family. Steve was raised in the Lutheran church and became Baptist when he married. When the divorce occurred, he quit attending church. "I tried to hide out," he said. One day his Baptist pastor came to visit him. He said, "We know your wife left you, but we won't; so come back to church." This was the beginning of Steve's recovery. Steve said, "If the preacher hadn't come, someone else from the congregation would have, they eventually would have come to get me."

Steve's account gives testimony to the power of a strong pastor and a compassionate congregation. For reasons of pride, shame, stubbornness, or embarrassment we found that young men rarely seek out others during times of crisis. They are like the prodigal son; they try to figure it out on their own. We also heard stories of congregations, especially in the form of older, wise men "coming to get them," being with them, and drawing them back into the community of faith. During times of crisis in young men's lives the Christian community has to seek them out. They need to be sought and cared for; they will not come to the church simply because they are in trouble.

We suggest the following strategies:

- Train older Christian men to become mentors to young adult men: develop a strategy that regularly places them in young men's lives.

- Do cross-generational men's retreat weekends or hunting and fishing trips, and so forth, where the old and the young can interact together.

- Do extensive premarital counseling in which young men can honestly face their woundedness. As evidenced by their stories, many of these young men bring family and personal baggage into a relationship. They are not always aware of it, and they are not necessarily able to understand and verbalize the issues without assistance.

- Provide mentor couples for newlyweds. Many of these young men and women do not know what a healthy marriage relationship entails, they need coaching from older and wiser men and women.

- Offer "fathering classes" even to those young men who are not fathers. Our research shows that young men are strongly influenced by their relationship with their fathers—positively or negatively. Fathering classes help them reflect on how they were parented, what they liked, what they need to work on or be aware of in their own behaviors. These classes may even open new channels of communication with their fathers.[4]

- Establish a relationship with a local employment agency and career counseling service. Identifying employment opportunities within the framework of vocation will address a number of issues relating to young adult male crises.

- Offer Bible study classes and discussion groups around the theme of vocation. Young men often define who they are by what they do. They need help framing their identity and vocation in terms of God's calling them into service in the world.[5] Douglas Schuurman's book, *Vocation: Discerning Our Callings in Life*, would be a helpful resource.

- Develop worship and community-building opportunities based upon schedules that are "young men friendly." We have witnessed excellent, creative young adult worship scheduled at unorthodox worship times, such as late Friday night or Saturday or Sunday evenings.

- Equip young men to do ministry with their peers in non-congregational settings. Peer Ministry training for young adults would be but one example, available through the Youth and Family Institute.[6]

- Offer to host recovery programs, such as Alcoholics Anonymous (AA), and provide hospitality in your congregational buildings.

- Build relationships with the local jails and visit young adult men in these settings. Provide alternative opportunities for them upon their release.

- Provide crisis counseling for men led by a "rescue team" of trained Stephen's Ministry or Befrienders older men.

chapter 7

SERVICE AND CARE FOR OTHERS

Expanding the Horizon

In his book, *Mankind in the Making,* David D. Gilmore describes the ancient code of honor: "The sacrifice in the service of family, this contribution to household and kin, is, in fact, what Mediterranean notions of honor are all about. Honor is about being good at being a man."[1] In this code, a man's honor has to do with taking care of one's own. Gilmore argues that men must be made, men are not born in a socially acceptable sense. Culture makes men and describes for them the scope and demands of true manhood. According to Gilmore, across cultures this formation process has to do with three foundational acts of service on behalf of family: sexual performance, supporting dependents, and protecting the family. At the heart of it is their "breadwinning role as a measure of their manhood."[2] A man's task is to serve others by taking care of his kin.

Gilmore's work is germane to this study of young men. Our young men reflect Gilmore's conclusions regarding the role of honorable service on behalf of others. A significant number of young men in our research wanted to "be good" and "do good" to others. Service was valued and had a local focus: first service to kin, then service to kith—those with whom one has primary, neighborhood, and community relations.

The young men are eager to serve and report satisfaction when doing something for others. They consider service both as attitude and action. It is an attitude reflecting how one approaches others and the world. It is an action of committing oneself to concerns beyond one's own personal interests to the needs of others. However, it is not a way of life that the young men describe as important to their lives, and it is significant to note how they see their lives as meaningful and respectable through service. When they speak of their conduct toward others, they often say they want "to be a good person." The language used by many of the men is general, speaking about doing the right thing and helping others, but for most, identifying specific needs and specific actions is lacking. It is generally assumed that a good person does service for people in one's own immediate context. That is, a good person serves their family, friends, acquaintances, and community.

Thirty-three of the eighty-eight respondents mentioned some form of service as important. Their understanding of service focused on being a good person, doing good deeds for others, and contributing to the well-being of others. The language and values associated with service include: honesty, respect, living a moral life, doing the right thing, helping others, caring for others, making people happy, wanting to "do stuff for others," wanting to give something back, and do unto others as you would have them do unto you. Much of this language reflects the honor code of Gilmore's research on the culturally conditioned objective for manhood. In many ways, it mirrors the Boy Scout pledge. The language reflects the values and ethics of civil religion—of being a good person who tries to do the right thing. It is reminiscent of the eulogies heard at a funeral, "So-and-so was a good man."

The acts of service described by the young men varied greatly: coaching soccer, teaching Sunday school, interacting with neighborhood kids, reinforce family values, being nice, congregational leadership, mentoring, giving gifts, financial support, being polite, honesty, making people laugh, participating in after-school Christian education programs, doing volunteer work, church service projects, food bank, tithing, soup kitchen, ministry with imprisoned youth, problem-solving, caring for the environment, joining a work crew, doing car ministry, ministry with older people, helping the elderly, being a youth leader in the congregation, working with a high school youth group, performing in a praise band, and participating in mission trips. Participation in mission trips as a past or present activity was mentioned more often than other service options. Often the idea of service was conveyed as respect for others without the intention of active engagement with their needs.

Tim

Tim's is a life of service. He is a thirty-three-year-old Midwesterner with a wife, a son who is ten, and a daughter who is eight. Work, family, and church fully occupy his time. At church, he teaches Sunday school, leads both a men's Bible study and a family Bible study, and he is on a congregational committee. Tim spends his rare free time riding his snowmobile, golfing, and racing go-carts.

Tim's teenage experiences shaped his values and worldview. He spent time on the street and saw homelessness, prostitution, and gang violence. He said these experiences made him realize "that there are so many people in need." Reflecting on his experiences, Tim places high value on helping: "You can't just turn and look the other way; you really should help people because they're suffering, and how can you let someone suffer?"

Tim spends time with his kids. He coaches his son's soccer team, teaches Sunday school, and interacts with neighborhood kids. Tim states, "Our home is the neighborhood house. We take people's kids with us to a lot of places that we go. If we're going out to dinner and the neighborhood kids are over, we'll take them with. What I believe by that, it is bonding with them, it is spending time with them and reinforcing with them family values, so, hopefully, that they don't choose the wrong paths." Tim invests in the safe and healthy development of children. He gains satisfaction from "seeing my kids being active, running around." Being around kids gives him a sense of "aliveness." What matters most to Tim is that his children "learn to be good people who hear the Word and go to heaven."

In high school Tim was the "black sheep" of his family. His family attended church regularly but he "didn't get the same experience as they got out of it." His life on the street led him to consider three life paths: he could become like the people around him whose lives were filled with violence and sadness; he could be indifferent to the hurts of such people; or he could "be the kind of person who respects others, wants to help other people." He has chosen the third path.

Tim's turnaround was precipitated by his marriage to a Christian woman and the birth of their first child. Their son's baptism led them back to a vital congregation with supportive friends and a men's ministry program. Tim is strongly influenced by the pastors in his life. He notes, "They have very much strongly influenced me, the teaching, hearing love, and compassion through them, through their messages, through what they do." His pastors' compassionate public leadership is important to Tim.

Tim's is a fascinating story combining suffering, family alienation, a Christian spouse, the birth of a child, and a congregation that combines fellowship, teaching, and compassionate pastoral leadership.

Consider Tim's life of service. First, it is not simply one service project that interests him, his servanthood takes many forms. Second, his compassion is based on firsthand experience of suffering in his community. Third, his compassion is concrete and action oriented. Tim serves children, youth, families, and especially men looking for open and honest relationships. Fourth, although he walked away from the church of his parents, the values of love and service were learned early through his family and church affiliation. Tim is "the real deal." He is a model of servanthood at home as well as in his congregation, neighborhood, and community.

Jeffrey

Jeffrey is a single, twenty-six-year-old inactive Baptist. He is a college graduate with a career in computer information systems. His work and involvement in the University of South Carolina sports programs consume his time and energy. As a booster of USC football, he buys season tickets, supports the university programs, and flies with friends to games. His immediate goal is to get into the MBA program at Chapel Hill.

Jeffrey is close to his parents and one remaining grandparent. He enjoys time with his friends and is focused on his career. Jeffrey attended a Billy Graham Crusade in 1985 and publicly declared his acceptance of Jesus Christ as his Savior. Jeffrey remembers it as a holy moment and acknowledges that his current relationship with God is not as strong as immediately following the Billy Graham Crusade.

Jeffrey has broad interests and values. He gains strength from prayer and talking with his parents and friends. He is most alive when hunting, fishing, or boating. He says it is his faith that keeps him going during difficult times and he believes that God would not put him in a situation that he couldn't handle. His priorities are that his job comes first, second is having fun, third is his relationship with God, and fourth is his parents. The values important to him are being honest, working hard, helping others, and not taking advantage of less fortunate people. He wants a marriage that will last.

Jeffrey is a young man who espouses the American values of hard work, family and friendship, sports, recreation in the out-of-doors, and concern for the less fortunate. He "keeps his nose clean and his house in order." He wouldn't "stab another in the back or be an embarrassment in the neighborhood." Jeffrey wants to get ahead and have fun doing it. However, his personal principles notwithstanding, Jeffrey lacks the passion for service evident in Tim. There's no motivating memory or awareness of hurting people needing help. There's no action on behalf of children: there is no urgency for a congregational affiliation and engagement in purposeful ministry.

Tim is a proactive leader on behalf of others. Jeffrey's sense of service is more parochial. He values helping others, but his sense of service and honor are more reactive and passive, more rhetoric and less thoughtful action. Jeffrey is ready to take care of his own, to be honorable and truthful. He doesn't imagine himself part of a larger response to familial, social, economic, or political need. It is enough for Jeffrey to hold on to God, family, friends, and hard work.

Going Deeper

These young men see themselves as caring people. Mike, age twenty-nine and married, is deeply community oriented, he helps others, including his neighbors and family. He and his wife give money and direct service to their community. He states, "It's just something you do." Jason offers a list of core values: not cheating, treating other people with respect, being nice, and telling jokes. Matthew, age twenty-two and single, supplies a long list of items associated with service and being an honorable man. He values the Protestant work ethic, being responsible, and holding on to the ideals of his upbringing: fair play, trust, being kind to other people, do unto others the way you would like them to do unto you, and helping people.

The young men more engaged in acts of service had personal experience with suffering (Jake, who was in jail as a teen and needed help to turn his life around), personal contact with those in need (Tom's high school years on the streets), or personal contact with models of a life of service. Tom, age twenty, exemplifies the formative influence of family and church friends on his values. He has been inspired by an older brother who is a former-marine and a police officer, as well as by the mission trips to Mexico he takes each year with his congregation. Tom feels good working in Mexico where he can provide people who live in cardboard-shack homes with sturdy walls and something other than a dirt floor. He speaks with fervor about doing what is right, being there for those in need, and stopping their victimization. His future plans include social service, medicine (his mother is a nurse), or law enforcement (like his older brother).

A number of men identify the way they were raised, especially the influence of parents and grandparents, as the source of their compassion. If this person was not a family member during childhood, then it was someone who has influenced their adult lives, such as neighbor, coworker, or friend. Eric, age twenty-three, values his grandmother's work ethic, generosity, kindness, Christian behavior, and lack of materialism. Scott, from Sacramento, California, was influenced and motivated by Jack, a contracted laborer, who showed such kindness that Scott and Jack became friends. Scott invited Jack to help others with landscaping and home improvements.

When young men speak of service, especially specific acts of service, ministry in a congregation is regularly included. When the young men offer concrete examples of service, in many cases either a congregation has inspired the value of service or has provided the avenue through which meaningful service was provided. It could be the preaching and teaching of pastors and other congregational leaders that inspired action. It could be congregations providing opportunities to serve as mentors, confirmation guides, Sunday school teachers, soup kitchen helpers, joining a work crew, or working with the elderly.

A proclivity toward attitudes and acts of service are anything but uniformly represented in these young men. Although thirty-three of the eighty-eight made some reference to service, fifty-five did not. Among those who understand their lives in terms of service, many speak in generalities while others speak of service in personal terms and are action oriented. The latter group gives examples of how service has impacted them. The examples of service varied from honorable demeanor toward others to direct acts of service.

Those who engage in direct action with and on behalf of others describe service as a powerful experience. The stories often reference the lives of others, their needs and their benefits from compassionate acts. Those who only speak of being a good and honest person do not describe these attitudes in a life-changing or meaningful way.

Although, some young men describe their service in relationship to the life of a congregation, almost none speak of service in the language of the Christian faith. Mike, age twenty-one from Philadelphia, is an exception. He is a drummer in a praise band and is one of the few who sees service as an expression of his faith. He tithes his $9,000 income.

Spiritual Longings

The young men who spoke of service made it clear that it gave them joy, meaning, and a connection with their spiritual wellsprings. This spiritual connection, however, was described more in terms of civil religion than historic Christianity. Nonetheless, the descriptions connote religious images that associate a way of life with the presence of a loving God. When they mention service, there is intensity and passion.

Other research indicates that service makes a difference in faith. Strommen and Hardel, reflecting upon the value of service in the faith of youth and young adults, observed, "An unexpected gain from involvement in service activities is an increase in church members' loyalty and affection for their congregation."[3] They go on to point out that youth in particular are positively influenced. "Service projects and service-learning not only bond the youth with their congregation . . . , but also enhance youth's sense of worth and significance."[4]

These findings are reflected in our young men. They often engage in service through their congregations. They feel good about their service and their congregations that support such meaningful work. What may be needed is a clearer connection of service with God and the call of Jesus to serve the poor and hurting. For the Christian community, service is more than a feel-good experience, service represents the life and work of Christ and his disciples.

Theological and Theoretical Considerations

Foundational to a life of service is the recognition of the "other." The Christian faith presents a vision of God's work in Christ intimately wedded to the common good of all. The well-known verse, "For God so loved the world that he gave his only Son," (John 3:16), expresses God's love for all that God creates. God's global concern is communicated by Paul in Romans 5:18, "Therefore just as one man's trespass led to condemnation for all, so one man's act of righteousness leads to justification and life for all." Followers of Jesus live out this work of God as they serve family, neighbor, and stranger. The

Christian message and the Christian life propel people outward to the needs of others. The model prayer, the Lord's Prayer uses the plural pronouns "our" and "us" and not the singular pronouns "my" or "me." All of what Jesus does proclaims and serves God's kingdom of love and mercy that reaches out to the lowly and fills "the hungry with good things" (Luke 2:52, 53). The kingdom of God that Jesus announces is clearly for the other.

The following climate of care and service continuums identify three distinct components of service: the sphere, the motivation, and the commitment made to others. These are factors in how and to what extent a Christian understanding of care becomes operational in one's life. Since love is a major goal of the Christian life that has no geographic, nationalistic, ethnic, or religious boundaries, the optimum point on the "sphere" continuum would be the care and service of the global stranger. The Christian motivation for care and service can vary from the narrow sense of Gilmore's male honor code (focusing on one's "own people") to an expanded human understanding of the needs of others, to a sense of Christian vocation on behalf of the world that is born in baptism and that lives "in newness of life" (Romans 6:4). Finally, the personal commitment to others can fluctuate from denial of the presence and needs of others to a fully embodied commitment that engages others through ongoing face-to-face contact with those who could benefit from strategic intervention.

Climate of Care and Service Continuums

Sphere/Subject of One's Care

Private/Family	Communal/Neighbor	Global/Stranger

Motivation for Care

Civic Duty	Empathy for Others	Christian Vocation

Levels of Commitment

Denial of needs	Tacit Acknow-ledgment	Conversation about needs	Monetary support	Study of needs for action and advocacy	Initial face-to-face contact	Face-to-face contact and action/advocacy over time

Figure 2

The young men in our study who spoke of care and service often used language indicating their sphere of care to be general and inclusive of "the other," including the stranger. Being a "good person" and doing the "right thing" opens the sphere of care beyond home or neighborhood. However, the motivation for care was rarely informed by the gospel of Jesus Christ. It was more often informed by the cultural norm of civic duty. The young men were generally motivated by their understanding of what "good people do." Regarding their level of commitment, most young men expressed a sense of care that was closer to conversation about needs than to real engagement leading to action.

John Westerhoff III notes the importance of service to the Christian faith: "Remember it was the life of Christians in the world that brought others to Christian faith. We are called to join in God's liberating and reconciling work in the world on behalf of peace, justice, and love."[5] Service not only expresses God's peace, justice, and love, but it also bears witness to those who have not been embraced by the work of God in Christ. Christian responses to epidemics and the needs of the poor in the early church confirm Westerhoff's assessment. Christians risked their lives and gathered those dying of plagues, helping them to die with dignity or restoring them to health with prayerful attention and simple nursing.[6] Their courageous care-giving became an effective witness to the substance of the Christian faith.

Care and service remain a significant factor in faith formation and transmission. Recent research on faith maturity pointing out the critical role of service activities has implications for the role of service in ministry with the young men in this study. According to research at Search Institute in 1990, "The experience of serving others, through acts of mercy, compassion, or the promotion of social justice, is an important influence on the deepening of faith. The evidence suggests that many youth and adults are uninvolved in such actions. Some of the best religious education occurs in these moments of giving, of connection, of bonding to others."[7] Whether it is the research of the late twentieth century or the behavior of early first-century Christians, there is common assessment that service makes a difference in the faith maturity as well as the transmission of faith to others.

Service, especially the historic and honorable service to family and friends as mentioned by David D. Gilmore, is clearly present in the stories and descriptions of our young men. The code of honor that includes fairness, helping others, and being a good person were often mentioned in our interviews. The frequency and the similarity of the language cite "being a good person" as a valued virtue. The challenge for these men is seeing beyond these generalities to specific acts of mercy that make a difference in the world. The challenge for the development of young men is to expand service in the name of Christ from kin, clan, and tribe to a broader horizon of care for the world.

Implications for the Church and Its Ministry

Although service emerged as a distinguishable mark of these young men's lives, it was not present for all of them and varied in its meaning and expression.

Social club or rescue station

In the 1950s, Theodore Wedel offered a parable that addresses the church's ineffectiveness in care giving and service. It is the story of an impoverished lifeguard station with one boat and a few dedicated people rescuing the shipwrecked off their dangerous coast. Lives were saved over the years and the lifesaving station became famous. Many people were inspired by the station's heroics and joined these lifesavers and their mission.

Local residents and those who had been rescued supported the lifesaving operations by building a new lifeguard station staffed with well-trained crews and many boats. The lifeguard station soon became a popular place for people to gather and tell stories of past shipwrecks and rescues. Soon, fewer members were interested in entering the dangerous seas to rescue the shipwrecked. As time went on, the lifeguard station became more of a social club than a rescue operation. Eventually, those who wanted to rescue the shipwrecked had to leave and start a new lifeguard station.[8]

The Christian faith is more than a community of like-minded folk; it provides love and service for the world in the name of Jesus Christ. Our young men are seeking a place of passion where sufferings are addressed and care, service, and healing are offered. Kenda Creasy Dean states, "Faith, it turns out, is far more likely to take root in the contexts of families, congregations, and significant adult-youth relationships—communities where passion is practiced, where people are given to loving others sacrificially, and where we experience sacrificial love on our behalf."[9] The church may be at a historic crossroads where the passion and compassion of younger people, in our case young men, is met by the passion of God to serve the world. It may well be time to challenge young men with the beauty, meaning, and joy found in the sacrificial love of Christ.

Service and care giving with a human face

Experiential service learning could provide a strategy for the church's efforts to reach out to young men. Like Tim in our study, others may be drawn to the value and joy of making a difference in the lives of others.

There is growing poverty in North America and around the world that is leading to a crisis in education, health care, and safety. Congregations in the United States have increasingly reached out internationally to the needs of the poor. Many congregations are reaching out to the needs of the poor in their own neighborhoods, rural areas, and cities. We believe engaged young men are waiting to get involved, and their involvement might well deepen their faith and transform their lives.

Linking young men face-to-face with the needs of humanity may provide the motivation that moves them to acts of faith-focused service. As Matt, an eighteen-year-old, said when joining his mother on a Central American mission trip for the first time, "Mom, now I know why you have been so passionate about these people for the past thirteen years." Matt's mother, Peggy, had been leading groups of Christians to El Salvador for years. Matt had heard of her trips and her concern for their welfare. She had been moved by the depth of their faith in the midst of difficult circumstances. Matt had heard all this. He trusted the sincerity of his mother's convictions, and yet it did not come clear to him until he met the Salvadorans face-to-face.

Mentoring relationships

Mentoring relationships offer significant avenues of Christian discipleship. Connecting individual men, especially older men, or small groups of older men with young men like those in our study, has great potential. Combining these relationships with service further enhances discipleship. Mentoring from other men provides a social and religious framing of service that can nurture young men's faith and expand their horizons of service.

Congregational internships, whether for a summer or longer periods of time, can be an effective tool for ministry with young men. Congregations can establish a summer volunteer service corps that works with needy individuals, households, and non-profit service agencies. There can be mentoring and training that focuses on lifelong discipleship. The term of the service could vary from a summer to an entire year.[10] The Lutheran Volunteer Corps has several ideas on how to organize, prioritize, and envision such a program.

Service projects

The compassion of young men in a congregation can be identified and gathered into a service project. Congregations can begin with the interests and talents currently present in the congregation. Service learning might consider a wide variety of projects including working with the elderly, the young, the sick, and people with disabilities; parks and wilderness areas; environmental and recycling; teaching vacation Bible school; hunger, housing, and homelessness; neighborhood health; international relief efforts; political action for human rights; peace; and social justice. The critical issue is that these activities must be linked to God's care for the world as revealed in Christ Jesus. Connecting care for others and the earth with Christian community is a formative approach to discipleship. Whatever the service activities are, the key will be the mentoring that provides training for Christian discipleship. The stories of those projects can be shared with the congregation in order to interest others in this form of faith formation.

Reflecting on service experiences, sharing the joys and challenges of caring for others, providing strategies and resources, offering support and encouragement, and framing the entire service learning activity within the context of the journey of the Christian faith are key components of this ministry.

Do ethical case studies with young men

Congregation study groups can make use of case studies that engage young men in decision making regarding real life issues. Encourage debate and questioning of assumptions and responses. Lead young men to wonder, "Where is God in this situation? What should I do in this situation? Where in my own life are there similar occurrences?" Explore biblical texts, Christian teachings, and ethical stances that relate to the case study.

chapter 8

WORK AND AVOCATION

"I don't want my tombstone to read,
'I never owned a network.'"
—Ted Turner, network television executive[1]

If the church is going to engage young men and their faith
formation, ministry might well connect young men's work
and leisure activities to the presence and action of God in the
world. Work will need to be seen as more than a paycheck.
Avocation could well be perceived as gifts, talents, and interests that contribute as much to one's calling as to momentary
escape from the pressures of life.

The workplace often generates panic for these young men.
They live with imposing time commitments and the pressure to
get ahead. The intrinsic value of their work and leisure is not
constitutive of their sense of self. Ted Turner's anxious image

---

of a tombstone epitaph speaks more to their experience and the internal values of consumerism than to a calling of living for the sake of others. Our research discovered few young men with lives anchored in meaningful work who expressed passion or calling. There is surprisingly little comment on the value of work itself. Repeatedly, these young men spoke of work as a means to a financial end. When reflecting on their work, they communicated little or no sense of satisfaction, no identifiable intrinsic rewards, and no dreams or aspirations for what their work might mean for themselves or society. Work pays the bills and is stressful for most of them.

Three of the young men in the study illustrate how work and avocation fit into the larger narrative of these men's identity and spirituality. Two of these men do not relate their work to their faith. God may be helping them deal with the demands and pressures of work but the work itself is not perceived as part of their life with God. The third young man is an exception in the study; he is a church organist who perceives his work as a calling. His story stands alongside the others as an exception to the norm and an example of what is a possible component of young male identity and spirituality.

Rick

Rick is thirty-one years old, married with two children ages three and five, and lives in the upper Midwest. His life is dominated by work and family. He is a salesman who has recently also started his own business. Work consumes sixty to seventy hours of his week. There is not much to his world outside of work and family. His church is an important part of his family activities. The biggest struggle in Rick's life is managing his time. Beyond his work commitments, family is his first priority. He bemoans that the rest of his time goes "down from there until the time is pretty much up." With the limited time that he does have for leisure, Rick enjoys golf and playing his guitar.

Rick describes his work as saving time and making money. With his two jobs, he currently feels like a slave to two masters. His work is both challenging and rewarding. He is hoping that his new business will allow him to quit his sales job. Rick's number one concern is his family. His underlying goal is to have more time with his wife and children: "Weekends, family is priority. I want to do something memorable either as a family or with the kids or just with my wife . . . makes up for working so dang hard during the week." It would be a bonus if Rick could have time to exercise and devote to his music.

Rick talks about work as income for his family and as a potentially successful business venture that could give him more time with his family. Rick is not bitter about his work. He treats it as something that has both pluses, such as anticipating more income so as to have more time at home, and minuses, such as, "working so dang hard during the week." He works to make other areas of his life more satisfying.

An interesting side benefit of Rick's work has been his boss who "is a devout Christian and is forthright with his beliefs." He says his boss "helped nudge me back toward an active faith." Rick gives evidence that work relationships can have major consequences for one's faith, values, and priorities—in this case providing a male mentor.

Tom

Tom is thirty-four, married, and lives in the sunbelt. He is anxious about his work. He manages a family business that provides income for his family as well as that of his in-laws. The concern for providing for both families "consumes" him. Tom says, "There's a lot of pressure to it when you're essentially trying to provide for two households. . . . Sometimes I get so down, I just can't motivate myself." The fear of economic insecurity is constantly on his mind. Tom expresses this concern bluntly: "I know what money's coming in; I know where we stand. It's a lot of pressure when you have that on your shoulders. I also know what money they [his in-laws] need to sustain their lifestyle and I know what I need to sustain my lifestyle. That's why it consumes me." Even though his wife has a job, he wants desperately to provide for his family.

Tom talks about teaching confirmation at his church. This ministry provides an escape from work. His leisure activities include fishing, being with his wife, spending time with friends, working on projects at home, and watching television. He adds, "In a perfect world I'd love to be a park ranger." Tom mentions this interest in connection with his love of the outdoors. The language, "in a perfect world," points to a sense of calling, to a position that would have meaning and purpose. Tom does not speak of "vocation" or "calling," but it may be inferred as an alternative to running his in-law's family business.

He speaks of God in other contexts. He points out that he takes his "burdens" to his wife and to God. Tom grew up in the church. When he was sixteen or seventeen, he faded away from church for ten years. Meeting his wife turned that around. Both he and his wife have become active in their church. She, in fact, works on staff as the youth director. Even though Tom is clear about wanting his faith to be an active part of his life, he does not explore how his work fits with his faith life, except through his prayers for help in the midst of the consuming pressures of the family business.

Tom notes that he has always had a sense of God in his life, even when he was not involved in church. He has prayed and knows that God was there for him. Coming back to church has given Tom a sense of purpose, hope, and fulfillment. Tom feels most alive with the confirmation kids. At the first confirmation camp he attended, he felt "really alive and connected with everything." Teaching confirmation is meaningful to him.

He enjoys "being with the kids, talking with them about their issues, getting closer to God, and watching them grow." He sees that God is present in most every aspect of his life—except his work.

Something is clearly missing for Tom. The stress of his work leaves him anxious and wanting more. He states this clearly: "This is my whole problem. I need something. I have the church and I have the kids and I have my wife and my dogs. I need more. I know I need more. There's something that has to help me get through it, not be consumed. I don't know what that is at this point. I need to create something or focus on something more." He suggests that perhaps he needs to work with his hands or have some other outlet. What he does not consider is that his work could be an integral part of his Christian life.

Jim

Jim's a twenty-two-year-old Easterner who is slight of build, a church organist, and holds a black belt in karate. Jim got into karate because "I got tired of getting my ass kicked." Jim is thoughtful, intelligent, and principled. He has a keen sense of who he is and God's presence in his work. He grew up Presbyterian with an Anglican father and now plays in a Lutheran congregation—a congregation that is his employer and his valued community of faith.

At the age of fourteen, Jim made the decision to be an artist. He observes, "The trade-off is I know I'll be poor." He feels strongly about his gifts and skills in music and art. He said, "At fourteen, I asked myself if I can do anything else. This is what I need to do; it is an absolute sense of call. It is a smack in the face to discount the gifts you are given. This was a decision of integrity." Jim has received support from his father who is a mail carrier and amateur musician. He was mentored by a high school teacher and his pastor who have encouraged him to follow his heart.

Jim's day begins with eating breakfast, working on his karate, practicing on the keyboard, or writing music. His evenings are filled with teaching music or a musical gig. He performs in country clubs and in New York cafes.

Jim is the organist in a congregation. He took the position as a job but the church has evolved into a faith community for him. "The relationships here gave me a different perspective," he noted. He confides that he loves to play at church. "Every time I play it comes from the same spot. I play what is true and say what is true. . . . I want to communicate what I feel and faith makes it less temporal." Jim continues, "Most of my stuff deals with love. . . . Faith is keeping love in your heart." He exclaims, "Dude, I like God and I want to say thanks and pray for something."

Jim is an example of a young man who has integrated faith, life, and work. He has a clear sense of vocation, a calling from God. His avocation has become his vocation. Music is his life. He has received affirmation for this gift from his family and others who have encouraged him along the way. His work as vocation gives him purpose (share music), meaning (express faith and love in and through God), and he sees it as God-pleasing. Jim could have spoken of his giftedness and interest in music as a special talent, however, he sees the interest and talent as a God-given calling. To walk away from the calling would lack integrity. It would deny Jim's sense of vocation.

The Broader Picture

The employment and education of our young men varied. Forty-one of the young men had full-time employment. Thirty-one were in college or graduate studies. Eleven had either quit college or had not started. Career goals were mentioned by twelve young men, mostly those who were in college and anticipating their future and hoped-for success. Seven men spoke of their desire to grow in their professions or careers. Four identified that they were at a crossroads in their jobs or careers.

In a few cases (six of eighty-eight), these young men associated their work with a sense of calling, work that has meaning and purpose and is God-given. One was a school teacher who teaches behavior management classes to youth who are in trouble with the law. Another was a nursing student who wanted to help people. One was a pastor working with kids in prison. Another was a highway patrolman who values care for others and sees this occurring in his work. All these examples come from people in service-oriented fields. Even in these instances, except for the two who worked in the church, the men's descriptions of their work did not connect to their faith. Their work was sometimes meaningful, satisfying, and seen as a contribution to others, but it was not perceived as a calling or part of God's will for their lives. One young man made a connection between his faith life and his work, but it was work that was directly part of the church. He recalled how a summer job as a church camp counselor helped him to understand his own theology of being saved by grace through faith as he taught this concept to others.

Sixteen men expressed a high level of stress related to their work. Three others commented on the stress of two jobs. Their stress resulted from the demands on their time, the threat of losing a job, apprehension about future job opportunities, difficult work relationships, and the overall concerns of the workplace in today's economy.

The young men had diverse avocational interests. Sports and nature were mentioned by most. Eight spoke of their interests in computers, whether it was playing video games, computer programming, or Web design. Seven played musical instruments. Five mentioned reading for pleasure. Other interests included: playing games with the family, drawing, writing, photography, group singing, dabbling in the stock market, dancing, home improvements, slot car racing, radio control cars, model railroading, gardening, and geo-cashing. These activities were generally and matter-of-factly described in terms of the pleasure they provided. Some of the activities were done alone while others engaged family or friends.

Spiritual Longings

These young men possessed few connections between their faith and their work. Most often, work relates to their identity and spirituality through creating a longing for something else, something more fit to their gifts and interest—something more satisfying, fulfilling, and definitely less stressful.

Stress comes from many dimensions of their work. An intense schedule often leaves Sean feeling that there is not much time for a future life. Fear of termination leaves others feeling rejected. A full-time college student who works many hours feels his biggest struggle is "keeping my head above water." For Manny, the hours demanded in professional school leads to a search for any life beyond study. There is the struggle of what to do after college. John wonders if he should get a job in the tight job market or apply to grad schools and incur more debt. Others vacillate between dreams of succeeding in highly competitive fields of sports or business and nightmares of defeat by the success of others. Other young men are challenged by the limitations of low-paying jobs. Hurtful relationships with a boss or co-workers or feelings of inadequacy make life painful for many of their waking hours during the week.

Parker Palmer observes,

> The soul is like a wild animal—tough, resilient, savvy, self-sufficient, and yet exceedingly shy. If we want to see a wild animal, the last thing we should do is to go crashing through the woods, shouting for the creature to come out. But if we

are willing to walk quietly into the woods and sit silently for an hour or two at the base of a tree, the creature we are waiting for may well emerge, and out of the corner of an eye we will catch a glimpse of the precious wildness we seek.[2]

The general lack of satisfaction with work suggests that something is missing from these young men's quests. If the "exceedingly shy" soul of these men could be listened to over time, perhaps their pursuit of meaning, hope, and joy could be charted and their "precious wildness"—their longing for spiritual meaning in the midst of their work and avocations—could be drawn out and addressed as vocation.

Theological and Theoretical Considerations

The lives of these men reflect what has long been observed: the workplace is stressful, demanding, and often detrimental to a life with family and friends.[3] The time demands of the workday are not only increased hours on the job, but also commuting time has increased as people live further from work. Job compensation and security have deteriorated with a decrease in wages adjusted to inflation, with the outsourcing of jobs, a changing economy, and company mergers and layoffs. The pressures are real, and optimistic outcomes in the job market are less than guaranteed.

Sylvia Ann Hewlett contrasts the recent economic environment with the 1950s, a period shaped by the 1944 G. I. bill. That federal legislation provided home ownership at low interest rates and an economy that required a smaller percentage of a single wage-earner's salary to own a home. Hewlett concluded that the 1944 G. I. Bill had "more impact on the American way of life than any law since the passage of the Homestead Act of 1862."[4] The G. I. Bill was the government's decision to support lower and middle class families directly, which had long-term consequences. By contrast, in today's United States economy, lack of security, higher economic risks, increased time demands, and more work for the same or lesser wages add up to a bewildering work environment that leads to high levels of anxiety. It is understandable how young men like Tom can feel "consumed" by the pressures to be economically stable.

It also leads to questions about an equitable distribution of power and wealth, an issue as old as the Ten Commandments. Walter Brueggemann explores the meaning of coveting in the Ten Commandments—"You shall not covet your neighbor's house: you shall not covet your neighbor's wife, or male or female slave, or ox, or donkey, or anything that belongs to your neighbor" (Exodus 20:17). The individualized and psychological consciousness of the West usually misses the true intent of this commandment. The focus is not simply on the emotional desire for something, but the taking of what one does not need that deprives another of what he or she does need to survive. The real meaning of the commandment is the concern for social practice and public policy, often abused by the Israelite monarchy and land-bearing elite (see 2 Samuel 11, 1 Kings 21:1-29, Isaiah 5:8-10, Micah 2:1-5). Brueggemann writes, "The Israelite vision of social organization, articulated by this commandment, is to prevent such confiscation that takes from the defenseless poor who have no economic or legal means to protect themselves against the economic powerful."[5]

Vocation and identity

The current, as well as historic, challenge of economic survival is a central concern for our young men in the workplace. The pressures and economic insecurities eventually prompts—perhaps even provokes—our young men to ask, "Who am I in the job market, where am I going, and what do I value and believe?" These are theological as well as job-related questions. The questions and faith issues that are stimulated by the workplace call for discussion of vocation, purpose, compassion, generosity, justice, hope, fairness, idolatry, meaning, and values—the list could go on. The church should be in dialog with young men on these important issues helping them develop meaningful and faithful work. Yet, it appears from the research with these eighty-eight young men that the Christian faith has not been effectively linked to work or avocation.

Concerns for work, wealth, and prosperity are not new. Luther addressed these issues:

> I do not say that a man need not work and seek his livelihood. But I do say that he is not to be anxious, not covetous; he is not to despair that he is not going to have enough. For in Adam we are all condemned to labor, as God says in Genesis 3 [:19] "in the sweat of your face you shall eat your bread," and Job 5 [:7], "As the bird is born to fly, so man is born to work." Now birds fly without anxiety and without covetousness, and so we should work without anxiety and without covetousness. But if you are anxious and greedy, and want the roast chicken to fly into your mouth, then go on worrying and coveting and see if you will fulfill God's commandment and find salvation. . . . If the heart expects and puts its trust in divine favor, how can a man be greedy and anxious? Such a man is absolutely certain that he is acceptable to God: therefore, he does not cling to money; he uses his money cheerfully and freely for the benefit of his neighbor.[6]

For Luther, work was not simply a means to a financial end. It was part of one's calling, one's vocation given by God. No office, no station, no estate in life was higher than another in the eyes of God. No form of work gave an individual a greater sense of righteousness or ease before God. It made no difference if one were monk, prince, or peasant farmer. All offices were means to slay the sin in one's life and to serve one's neighbor. Luther states these ideas succinctly in *The Holy and Blessed Sacrament of Baptism* (1519).

Yet in all these estates, the standard of which we spoke above, should never be forgotten, "namely that a man should so exercise himself only to the end that sin may be driven out. He should not be guided by the number or the greatness of the works. But alas! How we have forgotten our baptism. . . . So, too, we have forgotten about the ways to that goal and about the estates. We hardly know to what end these estates were instituted, or how we are to act in them for the fulfilling of our baptism. They have been made a sparkly show, and little more remains of them than a worldly display."[7]

Luther understood that one's work is a part of one's baptismal life as an act of repentance by dying to self and serving one's neighbor. The comments made by the young men in the research illustrates that these men hardly know of this view of faith and life.

Sabbath and life in balance

Most of our young men spoke of shortage of time—time for study, for family, for friends, for rest and relaxation. Their lives seem out of balance. They possess an underlying need for sabbath, a rhythmic time for rest and renewal. In account of God's giving Ten Commandments (Exodus 20), the motivation for the Sabbath day is Yahweh who rested on the seventh day of creation and thereby blessed the day (vs. 8-11). The God of creation knows the wisdom and value of a day of rest. Rest is part of life itself. In Deuteronomy, an added dimension to sabbath emerges. It grows from the memory of God's people once slaves in Egypt who had been freed by the power of God. Those who know slavery, know the importance of rest from labors. The biblical focus of the Sabbath is not only the individual but also the community renewed through the mercy and justice of rest. Dorothy Bass reflects this dual emphasis on sabbath rest by describing it as a time to be "recalled to our knowledge of and gratitude for God's activity in creating the world, giving liberty to captives, and overcoming the powers of death."[8]

Wayne Muller, founder of Bread for the Journey, reflects on our society's need for rest. "Our lack of rest and reflection is not just a personal affliction. It colors the way we build and sustain community, it dictates the way we respond to suffering, and it shapes the ways in which we seek peace and healing in the world."[9] Muller's words fit well with Luther's sense of vocation that leads one into the world on behalf of neighbor. Muller focuses on the need for rest and renewal so that work may be healing and just. He goes on to observe that though they are well-meaning and generous souls, community and corporate leaders are infected with a fearful desperation that is corrosive to genuine helpfulness, justice, or healing. Muller's comments on a recovery of sabbath reflect a consistent cry in the work stories of our young men. Muller claims, "Sabbath time can be a revolutionary challenge to the violence of overwork, mindless accumulation, and the endless multiplication of desires, responsibilities, and accomplishments."[10] He names the very angst expressed by the young men stressed by their work, "Sabbath time is not spiritually superior to our work. The practice is rather to find that balance point at which having rested, we do our work with greater ease and joy, and bring healing and delight to our endeavors."[11] His concerns combine the needs of our young men with the life described by Luther. The goal of rest is not only to be energized for more consumption, wealth, or prestige. The goal is to heal the world. Muller makes an appeal for sabbath when he writes, "In part for ourselves, in part so that when we go forth to heal the wounds of the world, whatever we build, create, craft, or serve will have the wisdom of rest in it."[12]

Implications for the Church and Its Ministry

In her book, *Big Questions, Worthy Dreams*, Sharon Daloz Parks writes, "Invariably, issues pertaining to the development of character and conscience—competence, courage, integrity, freedom, compassion, responsibility, wisdom, generosity, and fidelity, all qualities associated with exemplary citizenship and the best of the intellectual life—are embedded in our assumptions about the formation of adulthood.[13] All those qualities are also embedded in our young men's work and avocational struggle. In work and play, competencies and character develop. The workplace is in need of courageous thinking and acting on behalf of the world. Integrity is about the composition of life that brings existence together in a way that expresses consistent values and conduct. The freedom of which Parks speaks is freedom for—and not just freedom from—certain responsibilities. It includes being free to be honest with one's gifts and contributions as well as limitations. It includes being free to serve and create as well as to receive and be healed. Compassion, responsibility, wisdom, generosity, and fidelity are all qualities that come alive in work where one's thoughts and actions are tested and refined in the midst of social needs and possibilities. These human qualities can focus the church's ministry with young men as they explore their passions and talents in their work and leisure.

Christian Vocation

Christian vocation is a way of life framed by God's grace that is both gift and challenge. In Ephesians, Paul writes, "For we are what he has made us, created in Christ Jesus for good works, which God prepared beforehand to be our way of life" (2:10). These young men are called to more than personal security, whether financial or spiritual. They have been gifted as ambassadors of Christ. One approach to developing their Christian sense of vocation could be naming their gifts—their powers in the church and world—and developing them. Gift naming blesses and encourages young men to see into the future, looking beyond themselves to become more than they had previously imagined.

Mentoring for public life

It is difficult for young men to imagine a world where work and life are held together in the God who comes to make all things new. For that, young men require men as mentors (fathers, other family members, friends, coworkers, bosses, teachers, pastors, and more) who can present a gospel vision of life with words and their lives. Sharon Daloz Parks observes, "It is critical to remember that one can be mentored into the Mafia as well as into work that is morally responsible. The content or deep purpose of the mentoring work environment has great influence in shaping the imagination of the young adult."[14] Voices abound that draw young adults in directions contrary to love of God and neighbor. David's twenty-two-year-old brother-in-law reported that at his welcoming ceremony at a prestigious West Coast dental school, the dean of the faculty said the faculty and staff had heard many altruistic explanations as to why these students wanted to be dentists. The dean went on to congratulate the students as the ones who had made the cut and could now pursue their dreams of a dental career. Therefore, they could drop their feigned altruism and acknowledge that what they really want is a Porsche and all the other toys that wealth can buy. The dean certainly offered a different *raison' d'etre* than that of the Christian faith, one sanctioned and purported for men by much of society—wealth.

It is likely that a mentoring program where young men explore vocational options with older men of competence, courage, integrity, freedom, compassion, responsibility, wisdom, generosity, and fidelity will transform both the young and not-so-young. Forming trusted mentoring relationships, exploring Christian teachings alongside work and leisure, and developing skills and passions might well engage young men searching for their identity and place in the world.

The values of the kingdom of God

Jesus' sermon in his hometown of Nazareth speaks of good news to the poor and the year of the Lord's favor, that is, the year of jubilee that occurs every fifty years to return land to its hereditary owners (Luke 4:16-19, see also Leviticus 25:8-34). The author of Acts describes an early Christian community motivated by the economics of generosity (Acts 2:44-47 and 4:32-37). Luther writes and speaks of an economic order that is aware of and sensitive to the more vulnerable in society, those without the power or money to have influences in economic and public affairs.

Our young men—even those involved in the life of the church—had difficulty expressing how the life and message of Jesus shaped their understanding of God. At best, a few would say, "Well, of course, Jesus died for my sins." We believe they would benefit from getting to know more deeply the Jesus who was praised by shepherds, women, and the sick; who ate with, healed, and blessed those of low degree; and who died unjustly between two criminals. His story is inspiration for public advocacy by his followers of every age for all in need of hope.

Valuing non-productive time

Sabbath is for praising God and God's grace. It is rest for creation. It is about justice and mercy for individuals and communities. Sabbath is balance, health, peace, and integrity as modeled by the living God. Christian ministry can portray balanced lifestyles in the workplace and the congregation. Guidelines that encourage a balanced life in congregation, home, community, and workplace can be developed. Silence and rest can be celebrated alongside speech and activity.

Men's ministry as vocational center

A congregational vocational center could be staffed by elders in the congregation. These men and women would dedicate themselves to supporting young men to "become all you can be–for the sake of the world!"

The center would be a place with pictures and art of those who have understood their lives as calling. The ideas surrounding the notion of vocation would be asserted, explored, and developed. A range-of-life assessment processes, such as "finding your fit" or "spiritual gifts" inventories, could be available with trained people to interpret them. Life and career coaching could be available for anyone who asked. Servant leadership would be presented, explored, and developed through training and apprenticeships.

chapter 9

SPIRITUAL HUNGER

Spirituality represents the deepest level of the human quest for meaning and hope. Spirituality is associated with identity—who am I, and how I fit in it. Although not everyone would claim to be religious or even claim to believe in God, they are spiritual, they have a deeper sense of self and making meaning in the world. A person's spirituality provides a frame for the whole of life utilizing language, beliefs, values, personal morality, and public ethics.

"Spiritual hunger" is one's desire to authentically be one's self and make sense out of one's life and one's world. It involves a search for meaning in one's daily existence and hopes for the future. A person's spiritual hunger is expressed through a search for consistency and honesty between one's conduct and one's understandings of life and God. In the words of Sharon Daloz Parks, spiritual hunger "is rooted in a longing for ways to speak of the human experience of depth, meaning, mystery, moral purpose, transcendence, wholeness, intuition, vulnerability, tenderness, courage, the capacity to love, and the apprehension of spirit (or Spirit) as the animating essence of the core of life . . . it arises from the hunger for authenticity, for correspondence between one's inner and outer lives."[1]

For most people, God, or the possibility of belief in God, is fundamental to their spirituality. Since the vast majority of people in the United States (including almost everyone in our group of eighty-eight young men) believe in the existence of God, spirituality will be explored here as related to an understanding of God.

At the core of spiritual hunger is language, the words and themes that one chooses to express meaning and purpose. This spiritual glossary has dramatically changed in our time. The theological language of Martin Luther, the Reformation theologian who shaped the German language as well as Protestant Christian rhetoric, stands in contrast to the religious and spiritual language of our young men. Luther lived with an understanding of reality that included the indisputable presence and mystery of God. Luther understood God to be most fully revealed in the life, death, and resurrection of Jesus of Nazareth, the Son of God. For Luther, the individual, when baptized, is "sealed by the Holy Spirit and marked with the cross of Christ forever." The individual's identity is marked by Christ's death and resurrection and formed through the power and presence of the Holy Spirit. Luther stated that baptism "is far more glorious than anything else God has commanded and ordained; in short, it is so full of comfort and grace that heaven and earth cannot comprehend it" (*The Book of Concord,* Fortress Press, 461). Luther cannot imagine a world without God, even though he clearly conceives of a world that does not believe in God and the grace of God given through baptism.

Luther goes on to describe what many would consider a spirituality, a way of life consistent with his understanding of God: "In baptism, therefore, every Christian has enough to study and practice all his or her life."[2] Luther's spirituality is succinctly stated as the "study and practice" of one's baptism. His spirituality is grounded not only in learning more about God but in living a life consistent with God. In baptism, the reality of God that defies full comprehension has become tangible and accessible as a way of life. Luther describes the benefits of baptism as "victory over death and the devil, forgiveness of sin, God's grace, the entire Christ, and the Holy Spirit with his gifts."[3] His language is filled with an imagination of divine meaning for life and hope for the future, all of which describes human identity as a forgiven sinner sent into the world to practice baptismal identity by the power and gifts of the Holy Spirit.

Luther's frame of reference, his language, and imagery, are biblical and consistent with historic Christian faith, a frame of reference distinctly different from the language and description of the experiences of these young men. Their language and experience are more consistent with the results of a recent study of youth ages thirteen to eighteen reported in *Soul Searching: The Religious and Spiritual Lives of American Teenagers* by Christian Smith with Melinda Lundquist Denton. Smith and Denton note that traditional Christianity is being "colonized" by another religion, "Moralistic Therapeutic Deism," a religion that promotes salvation through most any remote god and by means of private goodness and happiness.[4] It is a religious takeover that few have noticed and has affected more than just teenagers. In fact, according to Smith and Denton, today's teens are merely reflecting the larger religious culture in America, a culture that appears largely indifferent to the influence of historic Christian. They write, "The language, and therefore experience, of Trinity, holiness, sin, grace, justification, sanctification, church, Eucharist, and heaven and hell appear, among most Christian teenagers in the United States at the very least, to be supplanted by the language of happiness, niceness, and an earned heavenly reward."[5] Smith and Denton go on to observe that "Christianity is either degenerating into a pathetic version of itself or, more significantly, Christianity is actively being colonized and displaced by a quite different religious faith."[6]

Smith's national study of youth and religion has parallels with our study of the eighty-eight young men. When these young men were interviewed, they rarely described their religious or spiritual lives in historic Christian language. When the young men who described themselves as Christian were asked how Jesus fit into their religious understanding, they either confessed ignorance or, at best, said something like, "Well, yes, of course, Jesus died for my sins." That brief confession, "Jesus died for my sins," is a worthy introduction to the Christian faith but far short of a full description of the gospel writings or the teachings of nearly two thousand years of Christianity. It is, however, consistent with a cultural emphasis on individualism, with a god that promotes individual salvation or well-being. This individualized, even privatized salvation, stands in contrast with the biblical reign of God that is presented as a communal event for an entire world.

Theological and Theoretical Considerations

It is evident that large numbers of the young men studied have drifted from the church. One factor that may be distancing these young men from church and the language of historic Christianity is that the church has been "colonized" by this generic religious tradition that no longer needs God's life and activity to support it. Whether from within or outside the church, cultural Christianity does look more like Moralistic Therapeutic Deism. The messages and voices that speak to Christian identity and spirituality in the United States may not arise from the church and its activities but from generally accessible cultural experiences. According to Smith and Denton, Scripture and the larger Christian tradition have managed to speak only marginally to American (including Christian) spirituality and identity. This is unmistakably evident in the eighty-eight men we studied.

Whatever the final analysis, it is clear that the traditional language of the Christian church has not formed our eighty-eight young men. Continuing to use the traditional language of the church is not likely to be the primary means of reaching these young men in their spiritual hunger. Their spiritual journeys and personal identities are, at the most basic levels, shaped less by Scripture and Christian tradition and more by personal reasoning and an assortment of personal, relational, and cultural experiences.

Hungering and thirsting for righteousness

Spiritual hunger is not the focus of conversation for most people, even in the church. Christians get distracted by and attached to other pursuits. Spiritual hunger is not the focus of our daily life activities, although it underlies most of our significant life experiences. It is not part of our common discourse, even our religious discourse. This is also the case with our eighty-eight young men.

Jesus spoke of the blessedness of those who hunger and thirst for righteousness (Matthew 5:6). What does this mean? To speak directly of the "thirst for righteousness" of these eighty-eight young men in some manner overstates the case. Most young men did not speak directly of such spiritual longings and yet, beneath the surface of their conversations, there reside the issues we have explored. The overriding message of the eighty-eight interviews was the openness and struggle of young men who described the power of relationships, delight in nature and sports, the influence of life defining experiences, the presence of crises and stress, the importance of service, and the quandary of their work. These men live with more questions than answers. Their questions are potentially life-defining and faith-forming. The lives and questions of these men are detailed in language that comes largely out of two primary sources of authority: the voices of personal experience and normative cultural experience. What is missing is the voice of the church—drawing from Scripture and Christian tradition—speaking in a fresh language that demonstrates a reality and a world rarely heard, seen, or experienced by most of these young men.

The quadrilateral in christian theology and practice

The "quadrilateral" is a helpful device for exploring the way these younger men frame their spiritual journeys. The quadrilateral is variously employed by faith traditions, such as the United Methodist Church, or by individual theologians, such as Lisa Sowle Cahill and David Tracy. The quadrilateral accesses four primary voices of authority for doing theological reflection and exploring spiritual life that are consistent with one's theological commitments. The four authoritative voices are Scripture, Christian tradition, personal experience, and normative cultural (including norms, various sciences, philosophy, and common sense).

Quadrilateral

Scripture	Christian Tradition
1	2
Experience	Normative Cultural Experience
3	4

Table 3

These four windows represent the voices of authority and sources of information that influence spirituality. They are four distinct sources of authority; they are also inseparable. One's understanding of Scripture is influenced by one's cultural and personal experiences and vice versa. Worship (Christian tradition) can be a life-defining event that shapes one's personal experience and reasoning. Nature can be experienced and understood in personal ways or through the Psalms (Scripture) that regularly presents creation praising God. Crises and stress can provide a normative and communal, even bonding, experience. Service to others can significantly influence one's reasoning; it can also define God's call. The call to serve in the name of Christ can lead to service activities that shape one's reasoning about what is good, beautiful, and true—even one's understanding of God. The four voices of authority interact with each other in a dynamic and creative way that form a person's beliefs and faith.

As authoritative information, all four "voices" are intended to be fully present and influential. For our young men, sections three and four (personal and normative cultural experience) dominate the "spiritual conversation" and influence their lives; their faith and life are often uninformed by sections one and two (Scripture and Christian tradition).

Even when young men directly reflect on their spiritual lives, what seems real is based more on experience and reason than on Scripture and Christian tradition. For example, their sense of God is shaped more by relationships and nature than by the Gospels and the creeds. Their theologies express the cultural norms of being a good person and getting along with others without the critique of one's own sinfulness or guilt in relation to others or God. There is little call to engage the world as a disciple of Christ—an agent of God's love, mercy, and justice revealed through the cross of Christ. The young men were much more at ease speaking about God in general or in self-serving terms (what God does or will do for me) than speaking about Jesus Christ and his claim on their lives. This was true even for those who considered themselves Christian and who participated in worship.

Our Young Men

Scripture	Christian Tradition
Very limited use of biblical language, story, or teachings	Negligible use or understanding of Christian doctrine including Christology, Trinity, sin, forgiveness, repentance, or sacraments; role of service as a Christian practice is a significant value for some
Personal Experience	**Normative Cultural Experience**
Highly individualized understandings of and articulation of what is valued and true "for me." Significant influence from personal relationships, contact with nature, crises, defining "nodal" experiences	(Science, reason, and philosophy) Lives are clearly influenced by a cultural and philosophy climate that focuses on the self, work, sports, consumerism, sense of honor, and parochial concerns

Table 4

The church faces a dilemma. In order to help young men hear and respond to Scripture and Christian tradition, it is likely that church leaders will need to start with young men's personal and normative cultural experience. The challenge for church leaders will be to hear and speak to personal and normative cultural experiences in such a way that these young men will also more clearly hear the distinct message of Scripture and Christian tradition.

This approach to forming the identities and spiritual lives of young men has implications for one's understanding of the church. The faith of these men, even for those who claim to be part of the church, is significantly influenced by relationships and activities outside the walls of congregations. It is through family and friends, mentors, and life experiences that the eighty-eight young men have "picked up" their faith.

When discussing the role of the church in the lives of these men, they routinely include their homes and trusted personal relationships. If the church is to reach these and other young men, it must see itself alive and at work outside the confines of congregational buildings and programs, in the places described in the "intersections" discussed in earlier chapters. It is in these intersections where men live their daily lives and engage in meaningful conversations and relationships with others and God.

Themes in the lives of young men

The young men described in chapter 3, "Relationships," gave moving testimony to the power of families of origin, male role models, wives, girlfriends, and children in the development of their spiritual lives. They expressed deep emotion as they described how these people gave them a sense of God's presence. It was not simply the words that these people spoke, but the experiences they shared—experiences of love, sacrifice, loss and grief, hope, simple pleasures, commitment to others, service, leadership, and living with the mystery and awesome presence of God. Through those experiences, relationships developed, images formed, and thoughts were shared that would influence the faith of these young men for a lifetime.

A larger backdrop of those relationships are the cultural norms and values that inform the spiritual lives of our young men: the need to win or "get ahead," an honor code locally focused, the importance of possessions and exciting experiences, justice narrowly defined by what serves the needs of loved ones, and an understanding of a God who "bails people out of jams." The voices of Scripture and Christian tradition need to be added to their relationships, sense of awe, hopes, and fears.

The "catechisms" of cinema, radio and television commercials, the Internet, professional sports, family loyalty, and peer groups can be expanded and challenged by including the Lord's Prayer, the Ten Commandments, the Apostles' Creed, and a grandfather's conversation punctuated by references to biblical characters and stories. It is clear that the last of these "catechisms" has not impacted these young men through worship and Christian education. Something more intentional needs to be added to their faith formation to help the young men wrestle with the voices of Scripture and Christian tradition. Instead of relying on conventional worship, Sunday school, and Bible study, our recommendation is to foster faith "laboratories" that engage the Christian faith within the larger, faith-forming relationships of family, mentors, and friends in young men's lives.

Life-defining experiences

The spiritual hunger of these young men often emerges in experiences that significantly change their lives. Congregations can accompany young men as they navigate these pivotal moments and reflect on their meaning and spiritual significance. While the nodal experiences of these young men's lives are serendipitous, rarely planned, and certainly not packaged, these moments can be wisely tended by caring mentors and hospitable congregations. All human experiences, no matter how mundane or sacred, call for interpretation. Whether it is travel, deep pain, a family passage, or a new competency, these moments are opportunities to engage these young men in their longings for connectedness, meaning, and life in the presence of God.

Some life-defining experiences take place over a long period of time; others take an even longer period of time to comprehend and appropriate into the identity and spirituality of these young men. What is needed is time to process and engage these constitutive human encounters to determine their meaning, value, and implications. It is the "over time" character of nodal experiences that offers opportunity for wise individuals and caring communities of faith to engage younger men as they sort out meanings and make new decisions based on their transforming power. It is not enough to offer a short-term course, a weekend retreat, or even a weekly worship opportunity without someone (a mentor or spiritual companion) or some group of people (a team or small group) to accompany the young man who is pondering the meaning of his experiences. Experience, as Luther noted, may be the school of the Holy Spirit but it is often an experience that needs others who are "called, gathered, and enlightened" to participate in the spirit's divine classroom. Such communal accompaniment in the action/reflection processing of a young man's experience can determine whether a particular nodal experience gains the weight of permanency in their spiritual journey or gets lost in the midst of a busy life.

Crises

Crises, stress, and the search for the balanced life are an open door to the spiritual hunger of young men. Divorce, alcoholism, crime, mental illness, loneliness, car accidents, physical illness and injury, financial calamity, losing a job, suicide, unresolved family issues, death, or chronic illness of family or friends can initiate or contribute to a search for support, meaning, and hope. These young men's search for stability and significance in the midst of life's crises follows a cycle of contemplation, fear, resentment, and awakening, as well as changed attitudes and conduct—the dynamics of addressing identity and a spiritual quest. In such difficult moments, the church can provide young men with trained mentors or host of mentors to accompany them through these rough waters. These mentors need to have done their own "life-crisis homework" so that they enter fully into these young men's struggles and point them beyond the shallow billboards of "You can tough it out," "Don't be a crybaby," or even "It's God's will." What is needed is a shared engagement of the mystery of life with a God who is with us. It does not mean providing easy answers, but pursuing steps into a future grounded in the hope of Christ's resurrection.

Young men can be brought into a meaningful dialog with the voices of Scripture and Christian tradition as they look more deeply at the questions that arise in these nodal experiences. This ministry requires much more than a clergyperson who makes a phone call or visit now and then. It requires a soul mate, a mentor, or a spiritual companion who is informed, available, and able to introduce them to a crucified God when they dare to plunge into deep and foreboding waters.

The framework of such meaningful ministry is a community of informed faithful men and women who surround one another with caring conversations and genuine concern. What is needed is an informed community of men and women with compassion who value authenticity and, at the right time, recognize the need for intervention. It is a shared spiritual quest that calls for uncommon courage.

Who dares go there? The church has gone there before and can go there again with young men. For Arnold, age thirty-three, who has experienced a lifetime of family dysfunction, the church looks like Barry, a compassionate Christian who drew Arnold into a men's Bible study and men's weekend retreat. Barry is an example of helping a young man in crisis heal, grow up, refocus, recover, and rebuild.

The balanced life

The parable of the prodigal son (Luke 15:11-32) focuses on the ministry response in chapter 6, "Crises, Stress, and a Balanced Life." It emphasized how young men either came to themselves and began the road of recovery or how others (especially older men) came to accompany the young man and help him turn his life around. The parable of the good Samaritan (Luke 10:30-37) is instructive as well. What stands out in the Samaritan, as compared to the priest or the Levite, is that the Samaritan stopped. The Samaritan saw a crisis, changed his course, and made a difference in the life of another. The Samaritan believed that his life could make a difference, that he could contribute to another's healing and hope. Our congregations can foster in men—old and young—this sensibility, this attitude, and conviction that followers of Jesus make a healing difference in each other's lives. In men's ministry, the church can reach out to the young who have fallen victim to life's painful events. Lacking such a vision, the church is most often on the sidelines, watching instead of entering where young men struggle with little help. We have seen in the lives of some of these men the good Samaritan stopping and intervening through retreats, men's groups, and mentoring that provided opportunities for deep listening, focused prayers, and sharing that promoted healing, hope, and faith.

Implications for the Church and Its Ministry

It is clear that the relationships described by our eighty-eight young men have deeply shaped their spiritual lives and hunger. Those relationships can benefit from ministry that addresses their real struggles as they work out their wounds, challenges, and dreams with the significant people in their lives. Through retreats, mentoring, short-term courses, service projects, and resources for meaningful conversation, congregations can enter the daily lives of young men to present Scripture and Christian tradition as viable voices that address personal experience and normative cultural values. Ministry needs to be done in a way that is not limited to typical congregational life and programming.

Engagement and action

Congregational programming has been too passive for young men. It has provided resources and instruction without personal engagement and action. Instead of providing inspiration and instruction through worship and education, congregations must encourage prayer, imaginative instruction, and mission where individuals, households, and even other groups take on faith in daily life. This model of faith formation does more than distribute church teachings, it assists young men in working out the critical issues of their lives with eyes open to the brokenness of life as well as the presence and power of God everywhere in the world.

Action/reflection ministry

An action/reflection approach to ministry values the relationships and experiences of life as important classrooms for faith formation. It is consistent with our young men's lives that are shaped by relationships, life stress, crises, sports, and work. It is also consistent with Martin Luther who stated in a treatise on *The Magnificat* (Luke 1:46-55):

> In order properly to understand this sacred hymn of praise, we need to bear in mind that the Blessed Virgin Mary is speaking on the basis of her own experience, in which she was enlightened and instructed by the Holy Spirit. No one can correctly understand God or His Word unless he has received such understanding immediately from the Holy Spirit. But no one can receive from the Holy Spirit without experiencing, proving, and feeling it. In such experience the Holy Spirit instructs us as in His own school. . . .[7]

It is in the context of trusted relationships and major life transitions that the Blessed Virgin Mary and our eighty-eight younger men encounter God in a way that becomes transformational. As "Mary treasured all these words and pondered them in her heart" (Luke 2:19) so, too, our young men can reflect on their life experience in light of the word of God.

Utilizing enriched relationships

The Holy Spirit regularly works through people and experiences to present Christ. Jim, one of our interviewees, attended a family ministry event in his congregation and went home to practice the presence of God with his children and wife, chasing one another around the kitchen table on a Friday night. Steve spoke of asking soul-searching questions that led him to be less harsh in his judgments of his girlfriend and to find a church that guided his quest for life with God. Jake felt alone in jail until Mark came with a Bible and a smile that said, "Have no fear." All of these moments are the "classroom of the Holy Spirit." Utilizing the quadrilateral, the church can begin with the dominant voices of authority that influence these younger men, the voices of their personal experiences and normative cultural experience and establish a lively conversation with Scripture and the Christian tradition. The church can provide occasions for their experiences to be addressed and challenged by the message of Scripture and Christian tradition through faith mentors in the context of every day trusted relationships. These mentoring relationships may be either short- or long-term, as long as they establish safe environments and with the young men. In order to do this, mentors must be trained and equipped to speak freshly and authentically of Scripture and their faith in the context of relationships.

Nature and sports

Congregations can use nature and sports to join young men in exploring their spiritual hunger. Adventure trips, retreats, and hunting and fishing expeditions can be framed by the Psalms, whose lively voices praise God with claps of thunder, with towering trees and mountain peaks, with awesome weather, with animals and sea creatures, with the children of the earth, with all that the hand and voice of God has made (see Psalm 104; 148–150). These young men can ponder that creation waits with eager longing for the revealing of the children of God (Romans 8:19-25). They can wrestle with why the awesome beauty of sunsets and rainbows are matched by devastations of tsunamis, hurricanes, and tornadoes. In nature, the lion does not yet lie down peacefully with the lamb nor the child with the poisonous snake. Let these men reflect upon the strength of Samson, the skill and bravery of David (the shepherd boy who would be king), a woman prophet who led armies into victory, a missionary who was undaunted by snake bites or crushing storms and shipwrecks, a warrior, or the Lamb of God who was slain and who alone stands against all evil on the day of judgment. Let them wrestle with the destruction of Ai and Gomorrah. These conversations will not be easy but they will bring reason, faith, and the lives of these young men to the edge of understanding and mystery.

Service

Service, like nature and sports, can provide an outlet for the kinesthetic needs of many young men. Service can also offer them a way to see beyond self to the needs of others. Helping young men see beyond their own personal issues can itself be healing for many of our young men who claim service as a value for whom it is more a general principle than a demonstrated way of life. When service is actively pursued, it becomes a component of personal identity and faith commitment. The church understands service as more than individual experiences and social norms (quadrilateral sections three and four, personal experience and cultural experience). Christian care flows from God's grace and takes young men beyond the interests of family, friends, and personal acquaintances. Face-to-face contact between the giver and receiver of care, as well as between the mentor and the young man being nurtured, provides a powerful means of promoting service as a basic human value and a Christian calling.

The church might well promote significant service experiences with young men that are reflected upon in dialogue with the voices of Scripture and Christian tradition. Ample evidence demonstrates that service is life-changing for the giver and the receiver of care. To maximize the impact of service in the lives of young men, Christian leaders can engage Christian texts and stories whose values go beyond the more generally espoused cultural standard of an honor code that is narrowly focused on friends and family. The most transformative experiences of service in Christian community call for more than an annual mission trip or service project. They embed young men in a culture that actively promotes emersion experiences and a community of respect and compassion. Utilizing action/reflection ministries of service can directly challenge narcissistic goals and values and focus on learning from all peoples and being a blessing to others. Such a culture elevates genuine respect and love for a wider spectrum of others, especially the stranger and the poor.

Work and avocation

There is need in these young men's lives to reconsider work and avocation as arenas of God's call and mission. Scripture and Christian tradition have much to offer young men in this reframing of vocation. Work and talent as honorable callings that serve the world and give dignity to the worker can be developed and used in men's ministry. Young men often get the impression that the only way to offer meaningful service in the church is to teach Sunday school, confirmation, serve on a church board, or clean up and maintain the church property. The Christian understanding of vocation in which one's work serves others and slays one's own sin has largely been lost. To celebrate the callings of garbage collectors, steelworkers, clergy, seasonal farm workers, janitors, dock workers, doctors, flight attendants, lawyers, and police officers as God-given vocation could be powerful. Society's cynicism toward doctors, lawyers, politicians, and other professions has been based, in part, on the assumption that they are motivated more by money and prestige than by compassion and service. The faith stories of these professionals whose lives reflect compassion and service can be inspiring and instructive for young men. One such person might well be invited to bear witness of God in their work each Sunday in worship.

The church can offer vocational guidance and pass on the Christian traditions of prayer and meditation. Imagine a congregation that helped young men explore their aptitudes and interests in the context of God's mission. The congregation could use spiritual gift inventories (that include more than just church work categories) and guidance counselors and mentors from various fields of employment who take personal interest in the career development of these young men. These mentors could be older adults who see it as their calling to recognize the abilities and gifts of young men and encourage them to use their gifts in service of the world. Why not imagine such an affirming, investing, and caring men's ministry developing the strengths of younger men?

The language of the church is not simply the language of Scripture and Christian tradition. That has been much of the problem for these young men. The church's language has become isolated, disengaged, and irrelevant. The language of the church must engage Scripture and Christian tradition with these young men's language of personal and normative cultural experience. A church that is open to dialog with other voices of authority is able to speak to a larger world with relevancy, truth, and faithfulness. Such a church can help frame the life experiences of young men with spiritual hunger in the context of a gracious God. As these men come of age, there is the need for the church to "come of age" by using language, ministry models, and strategies that address the real life issues represented in the spiritual hunger present in the significant life intersections of eighty-eight great young men!

chapter 10

GAPS

Throughout this study we have discussed conversations reflecting the identity and spirituality of young men coming of age. The dynamic forces that shape these young men are rich, diverse, and complex. As we conducted the study, we were more than a little surprised, however, by what did not come up. This may say as much about the study and its methodology as it does about these young men. For example, the format for our research was an intense one hour interview. None of these young men had ever met us before; thus, it is only natural that they might not speak of some things with a stranger, despite our assurances of confidentiality. Interviews were conducted in churches, and we are pastors. Church settings and clergy may have in themselves influenced the young men's avoidance of some dimensions of their lives.

What about Sex?

We suspect that because we were strangers, clergy, and interviewing in church settings, sex was rarely mentioned by the young men. Little discussion surfaced regarding sex, sexual activity, sexual experimentation, or sexual preferences. The topic was only raised generally, or in terms of regret. We heard phrases such as, "I was behaving badly at that time," or "I experimented with many partners." Those who went through what we have called a "wild child" phase, or a time of moral rebellion, alluded to having been sexually promiscuous, but little detail was provided. Even the young men in marital relationships never mentioned sex. Those living with a partner only mention the circumstances, offering no details. We surmise that had we held our interviews in a sports bar, library, or clinic we might have heard more about these young men's sexuality and the role it plays in their identity and spirituality.

This is not to say that sex and sexual behavior were not mentioned at all. In fact, when sex did surface in the discussion, it revealed the practices and moral values of the larger culture. Many of the single young men who were sexually active were living with their partners, had lived with them, planned to live with them, or had sexual intercourse without any marital or relational long-term commitment. There was little hesitation regarding sexual intercourse outside of a marriage commitment. Many of those who were married had engaged in sexual intercourse with their spouse prior to marriage. And those who did not have a partner seemed more frustrated than principled in their abstinence.

Gaps in Ministry Practices

While citing the "gaps" in our conversations, it is equally important to identify the gaps in the theology and practices of the church in its ministry with young men. Even as these young men are coming of age, the church needs to "come of age." Ministry with young men calls for the church to rethink how it does its work, its language, its styles of teaching and forming community, its practices of worship and service, and even the hospitality it extends. Although we found some creative examples of the church developing effective ministries with young men, much remains to be done if the church is to minister deeply and extensively with these young men. The term "coming of age" describes both the young men's processes of growth and as well as a call to the church to examine its language and practices and to implement new ministry strategies that engage young men.

Lack of Awareness of the Life and Ministry of Jesus Christ

Few of these young men have knowledge of the biblical story and its meaning. Response to this deficit was explored in chapter 9. Most importantly, these young men have little understanding of Jesus and his ministry. Jesus is most often perceived as a moral role model, "a good guy who laid it all on the line," or "someone who did what he really believed in." With a few exceptions, most of the men we interviewed had little comprehension of Jesus as a transcendent or incarnate being—the Son of the living God. What surprised us was that this was true whether the young man was active in a church or not. These young men are coming of age, developing their identities, and navigating the waters of early adulthood without an awareness of the substance and power of Jesus. They place their trust in a generic "god" rather than confess Jesus as Lord. In this sense, they share a deistic rather than a transcendent or incarnational theology.

As young men come of age, the church, like Paul at the Aeropagus (Acts 17), must find fresh language and symbols in referencing and lifting up the person and power of Jesus Christ with these young men. It is not enough to talk about Jesus in religious terms in our sanctuaries; rather, it is in the context of our "Aeropagus"—our arenas of today's public conversation and life—that the ministry of Jesus must be presented. A stellar example of what is needed was the employer who took his young employee to lunch to talk about the young man's life in relationship to Jesus Christ. This conversation within a trusted relationship had a profound impact on the young man.

These young men are simply not getting enough of the presence and substance of Jesus Christ. In post-modernity, when many claims are made regarding spirituality, the church needs to be clear that Jesus Christ is Lord of heaven and earth and is present and cares about young men's coming of age. Pastor Larry Clark, bishop's assistant in the Metro Chicago Synod, Evangelical Lutheran Church in America, has developed a most ingenious way of doing this in his preaching. He begins his sermons with a lengthy, rhythmic, cadence extolling and describing God, Jesus, and the Holy Spirit. He combines the Christ of Scripture with the Jesus incarnate in everyday life as he begins his sermons: "Lord, may the words of my mouth and the meditations of our hearts be acceptable in your sight, our rock, and our redeemer. And the people of God said . . . (response). Amen.

"Give honor to the most-high God, the creator, who woke us up this morning and started us on our way, God who is the father of us all, the chairman of our board, the chief priest in the temple of the world, God who sits at the head of our table, who made Eve in Adam's sleep and sent Pharaoh to the deep. Can I have an Amen? (response) Amen.

"Give honor to Jesus, whom we know as Joshua, Immanuel, and God with us. He is the Prince of Peace, the lamb who was slain, the bright morning star, Mary's baby and Joseph's conundrum. Jesus, the one who was foretold, the Logos, the Son of Man, the Word become flesh, the Messiah, the healer of the sick. Jesus, who gives sight to the blind, and ticks off the self-righteous. Jesus the way, the truth, and the life, born in a manger and ruling on high. Jesus the one who forgives sins, tells parables, and drinks water at wells with strangers. Jesus the one whose name is above all names. Jesus the savior of the world. Jesus the one who rides triumphantly into Jerusalem in a donkeycade. Can I have an Amen? (response) Amen.

"Give honor to the Spirit of God. Not any old kind of Spirit, but the Holy Spirit (can you say Holy?), the Holy Spirit who works down inside us, making changes to us, the same Spirit that moved over the deep millions of years ago, the Spirit who breathed life into all humanity, the Spirit who brings order out of chaos, and creates Holy chaos out of our orderly lives, the one who talks when we don't have words to talk, the one who comforts us when we mourn, convicts us when we sin, motivates us to love, that's the Spirit of which I speak, the HG is in the house. Can I have an Amen? (response) Amen." In rhythmic, engaging, affective, and exciting language, Pastor Clark describes the triune God. He draws people into the presence of God, even as he instructs the congregation as to who God is and what Jesus does. This explicit oratory gives a specific name and a job description to the generic "God" to whom many of these young men refer.

In chapter 6, "Crises, Stress, and a Balanced Life," we referenced the song, "Father of Mine," a lament for an abandoning father. This very real experience for some young men is mirrored in Jesus lament on the cross, "My God, my God, why have you forsaken me?" (Matthew 27:46). The mutual human experience of abandonment provides a bridge for young men to discover that Christ feels and experiences what they feel and have experienced. It provides entry into saying more—that abandonment is not how the story ends but that God, as a loving Father, reaches out to his sons through his Son and surrounds them in his loving arms. God's reach in Jesus Christ goes all the way—even into death.

We have reported that many of these young men pass through a "wild child" phase in their coming of age. They test limits and boundaries; they enter a "wilderness." The account of Jesus experiencing these same struggles living in the wilderness for forty days and nights tempted by the devil is germane. As Jesus wrestled with his identity, he was tempted with the misuse of power and the manipulation of God for his own purposes. Jesus' journey is similar to the wilderness stories of young men who used their power and freedom irresponsibly, often justifying their behavior through faulty rationales. There is a relationship between the stories of these young men and the Jesus story if the church chooses to build these bridges. As young men come of age, the church can also come of age, becoming more intentional in connecting the story of their lives with the story of Jesus Christ. This requires careful listening, informed reflection, and imaginative bridge building by pastors, leaders, mentors, and elders who are making these connections in their lives and thus capable of making linkages between the stories of young men and the stories of Jesus Christ who came that they may have abundant life.

Global Awareness

The young men in the study are not aware of or even curious about today's "global world." We conducted these interviews as America was invading Iraq (spring 2003). Young men were being sent into battle, yet these young men seemed strangely separated from the realization that their peers were going off to war.

In this age of the Internet and instant access to all things global, this lack of global awareness seemed all the more mystifying. Young adult men are the primary Internet users, yet their global horizons are not expanding through its use. Their worldview seems to end at the horizon of family, friends, and neighborhood. A few of the young men interviewed reported being profoundly shocked and moved following the attacks on September 11, 2001, but we did not find evidence of any emerging global awareness as a result. The murderous attacks of that day seemed to shock and disturb them but did not lead them to seek deeper meaning or understanding. We believe this lack of global awareness reflects our larger culture's indifference to the human community beyond American borders. These young men mirror the larger American culture that often lives in denial of or stands in judgment over other peoples and cultures.

Congregations coming of age and doing ministry with young men need to clearly reflect the global nature of the church. Our study shows that when this is accomplished, young men grow as well. Mission trips, global immersions, and intentional partnering with international Christian partners can have a strong impact on their lives. Congregations need to be particularly intentional in this regard. Even the young men who were active in the church did not make a connection between their faith and global realities. As one young Christian man put it, "I know I'm suppose to care about those things but I really don't." The challenge is thus set before us to link faith with global concerns if we want Christian young men of the world, not only of their "clan or tribe."

Political and Economic Awareness

Similar to the lack of global awareness, these young men seem politically and economically unaware and uninterested. They have a "small sphere" focus regarding the major political and economic issues affecting the world. Unless the issue affects them directly, they are unengaged. While many worried about their jobs and the great amounts of time spent doing them, they did not reflect on why their situations demanded such effort and sacrifice even while their job security was tenuous. Perhaps they, like many, feel that the issues are so complex that they are left powerless and victimized. We can only speculate on the reasons for this gap in our conversations with them. Interest in the political process and discernment of global economic forces affecting their lives were not part of their vocabulary. This gap begs the question whether an uninformed and unengaged young male citizenry can carry the mantel of leadership that shapes the future rather than reacts to it.

None of the young men interviewed who were active in the church mentioned their congregations engaging larger economic and political issues. Perhaps the closest ministry practice mentioned that addresses this gap was mission trips. However, we found no evidence that the "curricula" of these trips demonstrated analysis as to why people are poor, living in inadequate housing, or jobless. For the church to come of age in the twenty-first century, serious study, reflection, and dialogue around political and economic issues might well take place with these young men.

Institutional Connections

Reflecting much of the post-modern culture, these young men have little allegiance to institutions of any kind, especially the church. Nurtured on the cultural values of individualism and personal autonomy, they have little understanding of most institutional structures (unless it is a favorite sports team or *alma mater*). Their spirituality is personal, individualistic, and separate from the corporate, organizational, structural world of congregations and community.

While this gap reflects a much larger societal problem (service clubs such as the Rotary, Lions, or Optimists report the same frustration with recruiting young men), it seems to run counter to their dominant need for relational connections. These young men coming of age are looking for deep, supportive relationships with peers, family, and in some cases, potential lifelong partners. They are looking for the institutions of marriages, family, neighborhood, and community. Whereas they don't have many institutional connections, it is as if they know they need them but they don't value or know how to develop them. A number of young men who had spent time in the military, an obvious and formidable institution, spoke fondly of the deep sense of connectedness and of the order, discipline, and structure the various military branches provided them. Might the church provide similar institutional experiences that would carry over into the rest of their lives? We hope so.

We conclude that some of these young men reflect the larger societal bias against institutions and authority structures. They are unaware or do not care that institutions, especially congregations, can address their need for relatedness. Wise will be the congregation that recognizes their relational needs and addresses them directly and deeply. The value of critical institutional loyalty can be formed out of the experience of personal bonding.

Idealism

We were surprised at how little attention was given to idealistic dreams and aspirations. They are concerned about jobs, family, and friends. They are personally concerned to survive in the world, but they do not seem particularly interested in developing structures that might address larger issues. Only a few mentioned concerns about global warming, world hunger, poverty, or catastrophic diseases such as AIDS. It is as if their youthful idealism has been co-opted by a cultural value system that places expediency above character development, self-fulfillment above personal sacrifice, and personal autonomy above the common good. If they have dreams of creating and leaving behind a better world, we did not hear them.

The church has challenges here. In many circles in the church there is criticism of congregations that look more like spiritual niche marketers than places of personal and corporate worship and transformation. In their desire to grow, to build membership, or to appear contemporary, congregations run the risk of sacrificing their ideals on the altar of cultural compromise. Coming of age in the twenty-first century may mean that churches stand over against larger cultural values that are expedient, individualistic, and subjectivist, while at the same time develop new forms of ministry.

Our research leads us to believe these young men have not been challenged to think beyond their own needs or invited into a larger vision of life and meaning. Outside of finding a job, getting along with friends, and being a good family man, the expectations of these young men are minimal regarding the larger culture. We found that few significant adults have communicated to them that Christianity expects their best, that it expects them to "see visions." That is exactly what takes place through an encounter with the Holy Spirit. On Pentecost, the Holy Spirit descended upon Peter, and he proclaimed from the prophet Joel:

> In the last days it will be, God declares,
> that I will pour out my Spirit upon all flesh,
> and your sons and your daughters shall prophesy,
> and your young men shall see visions,
> and your old men shall dream dreams (Acts 2:17).

With few exceptions, these young men did not report to us that the church had encouraged their visions or their sense of Christian idealism. They were not called to a large life, to engage in noble work, world-changing practices, and transformational endeavors. We do not fault these young men in this regard; rather, we challenge the church to expect more of them, for we are confident that given mentoring, support, and a substantive faith, they will do marvelous things in Jesus' name.

chapter 11

PRESENCE, RENEWAL, AND
TRANSFORMATION IN MEN'S MINISTRY

A Continuum of Transformation

The young men in our study spoke honestly about navigating the intense years of early manhood. Their stories present the church with a challenge and a gift. The consciousness and lifestyles of these young men are not well aligned with the language and practices of the church's ministry. As a result, they are the segment of the population least likely to be present at worship or beneficiaries of the church's message.

What we learned from this study culminates in a proposal for the church and its ministry with young men. The proposal builds on what the church knows well and in some sectors is already doing. The proposal begins with 1) the individual work of a few men and moves along a continuum of imagination and practice to 2) new and expanded men's ministries and finally to 3) a bold new vision for the whole church. In this sense this modest proposal leads to radically new strategies of ministry.

Ministry of Presence—A First Move

During one of our interviews, when asked how the church might minister well with young men, Jeremy replied: "Do this!" By "this," he was referring to the intentional conversation of the interview. The research with these young men employed a one-hour structured interview that followed the content and feelings (message) of the young man as he responded to open-ended questions regarding his life, faith, and faith practices. A congregation would greatly enrich its ministry with young men by heeding Jeremy's counsel. We recommend four steps along this journey

Go there, listen, and walk alongside. One or more men in a congregation who are interested and able to genuinely and actively listen to a young man can invite young men in their lives and the lives of others in the congregation to conversation over coffee, lunch, or perhaps even a common activity such as jogging or repairing cars. During the conversation, be intent on receiving the young man's story at whatever level of transparency the young man is ready to tell it. Listen for the high and low points, celebrate their joys, linger with them in their sorrows, wonder with them in their questions, mostly just seek to better understand them. Almost every congregation has at least one person who does genuine and active listening and can help one or two men get started with this ministry of presence. In most cases the pastor will be able to coach these active listeners. We encourage the listener to talk at least five or six times over a period of three to four months with the young man he is getting to know. If the conversations and the relationship take root, stay with them. If the meetings end after five or six conversations, the listener might well continue to pay attention to, check in with, and pray for the young man whose story he knows.

Talk about faith. As he is conversing with two or three young men, we encourage the intentional listener to work with his pastor and other men to develop the capacity to speak naturally about what is true about God's presence in the listener's own life. This might best be done by honestly telling each other their own "God stories," i.e., the ways God has been present or absent in their lives over the years. The point is to become comfortable exploring one's own faith life and the faith life of others in an honest, gracious manner. When the listener becomes comfortable speaking naturally about faith in daily life, he can incorporate "God talk" or "faith talk" into his ongoing conversations with young men. Our research tells us that young men are eager for these honest, gracious conversations about God in relationship to what matters most in their lives.

Use the discoveries. Listeners engaging the stories of young men will learn important information that can enrich and better calibrate the ministries of the whole congregation. Without breaking confidences, listeners can provide the church with young men who can lead with concern, sensibility, and interest. In drawing them out, the lives of these young men will enrich the ministries of the whole congregation. This growing awareness of the worlds of young men will make them more present in the consciousness of the congregation and enable church leaders to develop ministries that better engage young men in the church and the community. Pastors might want to meet with either the listeners and the young men to better reach out to this disengaged "remnant" of God's people. Church musicians can learn from the listeners and young men what music best expresses and strengthens young men's faith.

Unleash passions, strengths, and gifts. Those listening to young men will soon learn of the great passions, strengths, and gifts these young guys possess. they will learn of the interest and need each young man might have in exercising these assets of their developing identity and spirituality. Over time, listeners might help each other become adept talent scouts, drawing out the best in the young men they get to know.

In addition to identifying and affirming these assets, the listeners can be on the lookout for possible linkages of the young men's passions, strengths, and gifts with the life and ministry of the congregation. Our study has shown both the enormous assets of these young men and their interest in exercising them—even leading—in arenas where these strengths enable them to make a difference. Out of a listener's quiet, individual ministry of presence could well emerge new ministries and more young men in public leadership. This would be a change that will influence the culture of the congregation and draw other young men into the life and ministry of the church. The Appendix demonstrates imaginative models of ministry with young men that incorporate these ideas. We believe you will find the "I-GO" strategy (Identify—Invite—Invest) and the "Together in Ministry" (Listen—Select—Empower) strategies of ministry interesting and helpful.

New Men's Ministry Practices: A Second Move

On a broader level, a congregation's men's ministry might imagine practices more attuned to the consciousness and character of young men. Such an initiative might well be guided by a small task force, perhaps called, "Young Men's Ministry Council." The task force could have two older men and three to five young men—some of whom may have been identified in the listening ministry of presence describe above.

Using what can be learned from listening to young men within and around the edges of the congregation—and gleaning ideas and insights from men's ministry literature—might initiate new ministries and practices designed to engage young men in a life of faith. The group may invite the pastor to read and discuss this book, *Coming of Age*, Richard Olson's, *A Different Kind of Man*, or Steve Sonderman's, *How to Build a Life Changing Men's Ministry*. From study and discussion, the

Young Men's Ministry Council can institute specific ministries within their congregation.

Men's adventure ministries

Our study has convinced us of the foundational role of nature and sports in the identity and spirituality of young men. Tapping into the interest, skills, and leadership of at least two or three young men, the congregation might develop men's adventure ministries that develop and promote weekly, monthly, yearly, and biannual events. These events could include mountain biking, cross country skiing, white-water rafting, water skiing, hiking, downhill skiing, trekking, car rallies, triathlons, international road biking, marathons, and so forth. Leaders would meet to select and plan events, sponsor clinics, develop funding, and promote physical and mental well-being in the congregation. Well-known representatives of these activities with Christian witness could be invited to speak in worship and clinics. Caring conversation, faith in life discussion, Bible study, prayer, and worship would be included on the trips. Men could participate in a single event or become a member of the men's adventure ministries leadership team. These events could be available to men only or for both men and women.

Cyber ministries

Nearly every young man "travels" in cyber space. E-mailing, instant messaging, blogging, chatting, gaming, buying, selling, arranging personal music playlists, and so forth occupy huge chunks of their lives. They form groups: the "gamers" who participate in worldwide online games (for some this becomes a way of life, it becomes their religion); "LAN partiers" who bring their hard drives and get connected for hours; or "chat roomers" who gather in Internet chat rooms to get or stay connected. For these and many others, the computer is the prime connector. Face-to-face conversation and cell phones have become secondary; most use the Web as their prime source of information and means of organizing their world. If the church is to engage young men, the church must "go there"!

Work done by listeners who have gone "face-to-face" into young men's lives, developed relationships, and identified the concerns, passions, and gifts—in particular with young men—can set up this ministry. Two or three of the young men who have been identified as computer savvy can develop a young men's Web site and begin engaging and exploring the lives of young men through the Internet.

All of the "cyber vehicles" identified above can become an entree into young men's lives. Blogs are more than about one's latest trip or question or idea. Bloggers often put their inner-most feelings and core beliefs into their entries, and anyone can respond. Care can be expressed, dialog engaged, options opened, relationships built, and healing provided. Beliefs and values can be shared through swapping and discussing music. Entire groups are formed through these conversations. Prayer rooms can be established at chat sites. Certainly, a Web site and a "cyber journal" or newsletter can become a prime vehicle for communicating with other young men in the ministry and reaching out to the world—literally.

Real life ministries

The young men in this study want to connect—to know and be known, to love and be loved, and to care and be cared for. Their previous relationships have not only not developed their interpersonal competencies, but have often left these young men wounded. We believe young men are eager to be real, show respect, and work together with other men and women. They want to become good people, lovers, spouses, fathers, uncles, grandfathers, friends, and colleagues.

Congregations and men's ministry's might join young men in their search for competency in good relationships and healing for their scars from the past through a variety of ministry practices, each with its strengths and level of risk. The first practice with the greatest potential for meeting young men where they are and carrying the least amount of risk is one-on-one "coaching" through practices developed by Befrienders or Peer Ministry. The second practice with strong potential for reaching more social young men working on relationships is "guy talk" or "guy and gal talk," although it comes with greater risk. The third practice with the farthest reaching potential and the greatest risk is to develop a men's life center with a full range of personal and relational healing and instruction.

Life coaching approaches to ministry intentionally equip older and younger men for personal relational health and healing as well as befriending or supporting another man in his growth and healing. Befriender Ministry,[1] Stephen's Ministry,[2] and Peer Ministry[3] networks exist that could provide excellent training for an individual or group of men who might begin such a ministry. Starting a life-coaching ministry takes only one man committed to such a calling among the men of his congregation. The coach's availability would be announced to the congregation, all the while the coach develops friendships with young men through a ministry of presence. As his work brings results, the word goes out, "There is a safe place in the church to work your 'stuff!'"

"Guy Talk" requires at least two men who will gather to work on their personal and relational lives. Weekday morning breakfasts, Saturday morning coffee shop gatherings, and weeknight snack sessions have proven good times for these conversations. Sometimes movie clips provide good jumping-off points. Regularly, men will just put critical incidents or relationships in their lives on the table for attention. Periodically, a counselor or elder can be called in for ideas and conversation. Peer Ministry training is a good way to equip a man to start such a ministry. "Guy and girl talk" utilizes the same format, but adds women to the mix.

Providing a men's life center requires much greater commitment and carries more risk and responsibility. Some congregational investment, staff, and oversight is required. Some medium- or large-size congregations have used such a vehicle for connecting the finest individual, marriage, and family healing and relational growth counselors into the lives of their men (and women). They have reaped significant dividends. In these centers, the full range of issues in young men's individual and family lives can be addressed. Counseling and instruction around singleness, marriage, fathering, divorce, pornography, abuse, chemical dependency, abandonment, sexual identity, and so forth can be addressed.

Coming of Age in the Church: A Third Move

In the first chapter we spoke of a new vision for men and women as "authentic, egalitarian, mutual humanity." The views of men expressed in this study, as well as in the other ministries discussed, have originated from such a Christian understanding of gender. As we have moved along the continuum of ministries in this proposal, from the least to most ambitious, we turn to a proposal for ministry with men and women that has in mind nothing short of changing the very culture of the church's life and mission. We move here beyond proposals for ministry with men to a major revision of the church's ministry with men, women, and children.

What if a congregation commissioned a task force (a "Coming of Age Men and Women's Council") to become ongoing listeners to men and women, young and old? In this council, information from these caring conversations, keen observations of the congregation's relationships and practices, plus the best literature on women and men's lives and ministry are carefully considered. The Coming of Age Men and Women's Council might be cochaired by a woman and a man and consist of a "gender specialist" and four other men and women, young and old. The council might meet biweekly or monthly to mull over two questions:

- What does authentic, egalitarian, and mutual Christian humanity look like?

- How might our congregation practice such a way of life together?

The council might begin by discussing *Coming of Age* or Mary Stewart Van Leeuwen's book, *My Brother's Keeper.* As the council reflects and clarifies its views, this information would be disseminated throughout the life and ministries of the congregation as ideas for possible implementation. What follows is a small sample of what could happen.

Worship transformation

As information regarding the unique and common consciousness of women and men is shared with leadership responsible for worship, the language, metaphors, and practices of worship could expand and gain a new edge. God is referenced using the full range of gender language and metaphors of Scripture, Christian tradition, and human experience. There is as much action and as many visuals in worship as there are words, so the actions and visuals in worship and in the worship space are fully representative of the worlds in which both men and women exist and act. The range of music in worship is as wide as that available in the wider culture and particularly reflective of that congregation's context. Nearly equal numbers of men, women, and children are represented in music and worship leadership.

Preaching is led by the clergy but shared by the laity, the priesthood of all believers. Regularly, women and men, young and old, "speak" in sermons through interviews, bearing witness, asking questions, sharing art, telling stories, and engaging in dialog. The issues addressed and illustrations appearing in sermons become more concrete, true to life, representative of the full life struggle of men and women of every age—especially those in the community surrounding the congregation. The sermon is as much action, visual, drama, and media as it is words—oration or essay.

The prayers of the church reflect petitions flowing from the gladness and groaning in the hearts of all women, men, and children as they "work their lives" and as others around the world "work their lives" during that particular week. With permission gained, the prayers reflect more the concrete, human pathos spoken in an Alcoholics Anonymous meeting than of a religious pageant.

Worship leadership, while representing a wide range of women, men, and children, would most often be shared by people of both genders collaborating in the sharing of power between men and women and laity and clergy.

Worship services introduce a new practice or segment called "martyria," which means, "witness," "faith in daily life," or "God-bearers." In this short segment, women, men, and children would speak of life as a calling, particularly as they exercise that vocation in the particular places where they live and serve God.

Coming of age milestones

A milestone is a meaningful, memorable moment in a person or community's life. Coming of age milestones celebrate meaningful, memorable moments at specific stages of development for men and women. These milestones promote growth in faith and life at those pivotal occasions. Each coming of age milestone will bring the generations together around young men and women to form their lives as the congregation explores their gifts, discipleship, future life stories, and equips them through spiritual mentors, and a faith community of support. The format includes the following:

- Faith formation and cross-generational enrichment groups

- Worship celebrations

- Community gatherings

- Mentors

- Follow-up support

- Establishment of practices and rituals

Youth and Family Institute's[4] *Milestones Ministry* materials or the *Journey to Adulthood* curriculum from the Episcopal Church in the United States could be used in "Coming of Age Roundtables" convened for both young men and women at ages twelve to fourteen, sixteen and seventeen, and twenty-four and twenty-five. The "roundtables" would consist of six to eight significant people in the young person's life and would participate in developing for each young woman or man a life strengths map, a mission statement, and a future story. They would also be an advisory council and serve as spiritual companions.

Each "roundtable" would culminate in a commissioning service of the young person that is integrated into Sunday morning worship.

Life vocation center

The life vocation center would be staffed largely by retired men and women of the congregation. These elders would dedicate themselves to supporting young women and men to "become all you can be in Jesus Christ for the sake of the world!"

The life vocation center would occupy a space filled with pictures and art of those who have understood their lives as a calling. The rich ideas surrounding the notion of vocation would be asserted, explored, and developed. A range of life assessment processes, such as "Finding Your Fit" and "Spiritual

Gifts Inventory,"[5] would be available with seasoned people to interpret them. Life and career coaching would be available for anyone who asked for it. Job search and employment assistance would be offered. Servant leadership would be presented, explored, and developed through training and apprenticeship.

Collaborative leadership

The Coming of Age Men and Women's Council, working with each ministry in the congregation, might wonder about the impact of gender considerations on the life of the entire congregation. Starting in the earliest years of the first third of life, attention would be given to mutual male and female leadership in the nursery with the youngest of infants on through childhood, youth, adulthood, and "elderhood."

Perhaps there would be as many men working in the nursery as women. Perhaps the nursery would have as many "action spaces" as cribs and rocking chairs. Women and men can stand shoulder-to-shoulder in nearly even numbers throughout all children's and youth and family ministries including Sunday school, confirmation, and youth ministry. There might be as many women as men on church councils, finance committees, and in the pulpit. Perhaps there would be a young women's and a young men's adventure corps led by adults of the same gender. Providing some same sex activities is as important as providing both men and women's soccer at school—especially during the early years of puberty.

The deliberations of the Coming of Age Men and Women's Council would go on month after month as they pushed the boundaries of the role of gender in the theology and the mission of the church, all the while carrying on conversation about their discoveries with ministry leaders throughout the congregation.

Young Men and the Church

"Where have all the young men gone?" Working this question that gave birth to this project would be a contribution to the church as it readies itself for ministry in the twenty-first century. The young men we met have led us to believe this is so. We found in the mystery of their lives interesting stirrings and struggles as well as challenges and gifts that both they and the church might engage on their paths to greater maturity. We are honored to have received their stories and share them with others, and to wonder with leaders about the role of the church in their lives and the lives of other men of their generation!

APPENDIX

A Vision for Young Men's Ministry

Lutheran Men in Mission (LMM), the men's ministry of the Evangelical Lutheran Church in America (ELCA), has noticed something that many of us would like to ignore: many young men ages eighteen to twenty-four are not connected with God through Jesus Christ because they can't connect with our existing churches. Young men are the age and gender group most absent from Christian faith communities. Why is that, and what can we do?

It has been the assumption that young men will return to churches when they settle down, get married, and have kids. For many years, this was true to a certain extent. But we are entering a time when young men have nowhere to return to. They never were a part of a community of believers.

At the same time, major shifts are taking place within society and culture as to how people, especially young people, see the world. Many times these new and different ways of understanding life conflict with values and structures on which our churches are based. Therefore, there is something deep down that just doesn't seem right about many churches to young men. And it goes much deeper than the style of music.

From their perspective, it doesn't make sense to expect young men to come to our existing worship gatherings or men's ministries. Nor will it work to try to develop a new and better program and hope young men show up. We need to put to rest the "you-come-to-us" model and deeply invest in a "we-will-go-to-you" model. The church needs to be sent out into the world.

What does this look like? When we look across the country in our congregations, we see men who have walked with the Lord for more than half a century—men who have stayed married to the same woman for forty years, men who have the wisdom of many years lived, and men who are by no means perfect but who are willing to share their lives. These men have something young men need. Recent research sponsored by LMM shows that fathers and other older men in a young man's life are the most significant factors in shaping their adult spiritual identity. However, sometimes these men do not realize how much they have to offer and how much they are needed.

But what if these men—these men who know what it means to walk with the Lord, these men who have the wisdom of many years lived—were empowered to go to where young men are and build relationships? What if the men in our congregations caught a vision of the impact they could have on a young man? What if the lives of young men all over the country were being changed because men of God were taking risks and accepting the call to invest in the life of one young man?

How does this start? There are a number of ways to go about building relationships with young men. Included in this book are two models to help you start thinking about what would work for your context and to empower you to make it happen.

We cannot expect young men to just show up at our church buildings. We need to go to them. And that means you need to build authentic relationships. God is raising up the men of our church to invest in the lives of young men. You are needed. Will you go?

"I-Go": Identify—Invite—Invest

The "I-Go" model is a simple, organic strategy that provides a three-step process for building relationships with young men. It is based on the three "I"s of relationship building (identifying, inviting, and investing) and upon the conviction that "I will go" and do this. In this model, you don't have to wait to get going. You just go and do it.

Identify

What young man has God put in your life? With whom do you have a natural connection—a grandson, an employee? Perhaps it's the guy who works at the clubhouse, your neighbor, or your friend's son. Whoever it is, identify a young man with whom you can connect.

Invite

Take a risk and get to know him. Ask questions. Find out what makes him come alive. Invite him into conversation. Then invite him to do something with you. Maybe it is fishing, maybe it is dinner. Make use of shared interests.

Invest

Develop an ongoing relationship with the young man. Have a biweekly Bible study, a weekly golf outing, a monthly time to work on cars together, or a regular invitation to have supper together. Find something that works for you. As you do something together, learn his story and share yours. Listen and be real. Live your life transparently and honestly, allowing him to see the real you. Let meaningful conversations just happen. Watch as God changes both of you.

"I-Go"

Young men need a man to listen to them, to believe in them, and to model what life looks like with God. Identify. Invite. Invest. Keep it simple. Just build a relationship with a young man. You don't have to be perfect. You just need to be you; you just need to go to them. God is going to do great things through you!

Together in Ministry: Listen—Select—Empower

One model that has worked on a national level with LMM is to intentionally listen to young men, select a few with leadership potential, and then empower them to design and implement ministries with you. "Together in Ministry" works best using a team of men to carry out the three steps.

Listen!

Start by gathering a team of men (age forty and above) to listen to young men in a non-judgmental way. The purpose of these conversations is to start relationships and to gain an understanding of the men you are engaging in conversation. The purpose at this point is not necessarily to involve them in any activity in the congregation. Select men age eighteen to thirty-four who are members of the congregation, but not active. Also include men who are not members. If possible, be sure the group represents various ethnic backgrounds and ages.

Referrals for these conversations may come from your pastor or church directory, family and friend relationships, and other young men with whom you talk.

Invite a young man to lunch or dinner and let him know you would like to get to know him better. When you meet, thank him for getting together and share a small story about yourself to set the tone of the conversation. Then tell him why you are interviewing him: "We miss young men in our church. Obviously, you are not coming for a good reason and I can respect that. What I really want to do is hear a bit more about who you are, just as you are."

The conversations should take place in a casual setting outside the church building, such as a coffee shop. Also, have these conversations one-on-one or as a team of two so as to not overwhelm him with a whole group of church leaders.

Use the following questions as a guide for you to help initiate conversation and get to know the young man. Do not use these suggestions as a strict interview outline.

Listen to life experience

1. Describe to me your life situation at the moment.
2. How do you spend your time on weekdays, evenings, weekends?
3. What are your most enjoyable leisure activities?
4. What TV shows do you watch?
5. What type of music do you listen to?
6. How do you spend your income?
7. Who are the people most active in your relationship life right now?
8. Tell me about your family relationships and how they are going for you.
9. Describe a recent experience with friends or family that was meaningful for you.
10. What issue are you currently struggling with?

Listen to spirituality

1. Thinking back on your life, what were some events that helped to shape who you are now?
2. Tell me about some people who strongly influenced you.
3. What really matters most to you?
4. What are some values or principles that are important to you?
5. What moments in your life would you describe as being meaningful?
6. Describe an event in your past that you would name as being spiritual in some way.
7. What are some of your biggest hopes for the future?
8. What are your thoughts about God as a "higher power"?

Listen to faith practices

1. What refreshes you or gives you strength?
2. What makes you feel really alive?
3. What keeps you going when things are difficult?
4. What is a balanced life for you?
5. What do you do to get centered, to gain focus in your life?
6. When or where do you have a sense of peace?
7. What are your feelings about religion?
8. If you had one message for the men's ministry leaders in our congregation, what would it be?

Select!

Gather together as a leadership team after you have conducted a number of interviews. Without sharing names, discuss the following:

1. What were the common themes of your conversations?
2. What surprised you?
3. How are your men's ministry and congregation dealing with the common themes?

Among those you spoke with, who demonstrated leadership capabilities?
1. Who was able to articulate his concerns?
2. Who seems to be a person other guys would follow?
3. Who has some sense of what the church needs to be about in order to reach this generation?

Invite two to four of those with leadership potential to meet with your leadership team.

Empower!

1. Share your notes from the last meeting, telling the younger men what you think you heard and ask them for validation or correction.
2. When you have been assured that you have heard what the young men were saying, talk about the kind of activities, programs, ministries, and relationships that will deal with the issues and themes they mentioned.
3. With newsprint, cluster the themes and issues that surfaced.
4. What do the young men think are the most crucial issues to deal with first?
5. What is needed to address these issues?
6. How, who, when?

Remember, the point of these conversations and evaluation sessions is not for the older men to provide programs and ministries for younger men, it is to give permission and empower younger men to develop a ministry—along with middle-age and older men.

Many young men will be suspicious of what you want from them. You must earn their trust. As you do, be open to what ministry with young men looks like and make it happen together!

Why Build Intergenerational Relationships?

1. Young men are the group most disconnected from Christian communities.
2. Young men say they want older men in their lives.
3. Faith and what it means to be a man is passed down from one man to another.
4. Many young men don't have fathers because of divorce, death, or because the father is absent emotionally and spiritually.
5. Many young men don't have extended family nearby.
6. Many young men don't trust institutions or organized religion. Faith and masculinity must be passed down organically through relationships. Young men must witness real men live real lives (in all its messiness) with the real Jesus.
7. Many young men are confused over the difference between the way the world should be (the way they want it to be) and the way the world is. Intergenerational relationships can provide some clarity amid the confusion.
8. Young men have a sense that at some point they will need to step up and make a difference. In other generations, this was more defined. Now, young men wonder, how, why, and can I? Intergenerational relationships can help answer these questions.
9. Older men are blessed with experience and wisdom to be a blessing. They get to make a difference in young men's lives.
10. Young men can be a wonderful blessing in the lives of older men, bringing new purpose, life, and energy.

ENDNOTES

Ch. 1: Exploring the Identity and Spirituality of Younger Men

1. Craig Kennet Miller, *Postmoderns: The Beliefs, Hopes, and Fears of Young Americans* (Nashville: Discipleship Resources, 1996), 164.
2. Ibid.
3. Ibid.
4. Gail Malmgreen, "Domestic Discords: Women and the Family in East Cheshire Methodism, 1750–1830," in *Disciplines of Faith: Studies in Religion, Patriarchy and Politics* (London: Routledge and Kegan Paul, 1987), 56.
5. Michael Argyle, *Religious Behaviour* (London: Routledge and Kegan Paul, 1958), 76.
6. The Barna Group, Women Are the Backbone of Christian Congregations in America. www.barna.org/FlexPage.aspx?Page=Barna Update&BarnaUpdateId=47 (2000).
7. Conrad Cherry, Betty Deberg, and Amanda Porterfield. Quoted in "The Spirit of Education" by Mary Heer-Forsberg in *The Lawlor Review*, (Winter 2002, vol. 10, no. 2), 15.

Ch. 2: Young Men and Ministry

1. Ann Douglas, *The Feminization of American Culture* (New York: Doubleday, 1977), 97.
2. Quoted in Milton Powell, ed., *The Voluntary Church: American Religious Life Seen through the Eyes of European Visitors* (New York and London: Macmillan, 1866), 69.

3. Eliza Farnham, *Woman and Her Era* (New York: C.M. Plumb and Co., 1864), 95.
4. Michael Kimmel, *Manhood in America* (New York: The Free Press, 1996), 176.
5. Ibid.
6. Mary Stewart Van Leeuwen, *My Brother's Keeper* (Downers Grove: InterVarsity Press, 2002), 154.
7. Nancy Maclean, *Behind the Mask of Chivalry* (New York: Oxford University Press, 1995), 161.
8. Kimmel, 179.
9. Van Leeuwen, 43.
10. Ibid., 44.

Ch. 3: Relationships

1. Miller, 16.
2. Ibid., 165.
3. Stephen C. Barton, ed., *The Family in Theological Perspective,* (Edinburgh: T&T Clark), 5.
4. Ibid., 6.

Ch. 4: Nature and Sports

1. Sharon Daloz Parks, *Big Questions, Worthy Dreams* (San Francisco: Jossey-Bass, 2000), 189.
2. David Walsh, *Why Do They Act That Way?* (New York: The Free Press, 2004), 97.
3. Ibid., 98.

Ch. 5: Life-Defining Experiences

1. *The World Book Dictionary* (Chicago: World Book, Inc., 1989), 1410-11.
2. Peter Mayer, *Stirring Up the Water: Songs of Faith* (Little Flock Music, 2003).
3. David Moshman, *Adolescent Psychological Development* (London, N. J.: Lawrence Erlbaum Associates, 2005), 83.
4. Ibid., 85.
5. Ibid., 84.
6. Ibid., 83.

Ch. 6: Crises, Stress, and a Balanced Life

1. Simon Baron-Cohen, *The Essential Difference* (New York: Basic Books, 2003), 93.

2. Martin Luther, *Luther's Large Catechism,* (Minneapolis: Augsburg Fortress Publishing House, 1967), 38.

3. Dietrich Bonhoeffer, *Christ the Center* (New York: Harper and Row, 1960), 62.

4. We suggest exploring the Boys Town curriculum catalog at http://www.boystownpress.org and the Augsburg Fortress Web site at http://www.augsburgfortress.org for resource suggestions.

5. Douglas J. Schuurman, *Vocation: Discerning Our Callings in Life* (Grand Rapids, Mich.: William B. Eerdman's Publishing Company, 2004).

6. www.youthandfamilyinstitute.org

Ch. 7: Service and Care for Others

1. David D. Gilmore, *Mankind in the Making* (New Haven: Yale University Press, 1990), 43.

2. Ibid.

3. Merton P. Strommen and Richard A. Hardel, *Passing on the Faith: A Radical New Model for Youth and Family Ministry* (Winona, Minn.: St. Mary's Press, 2000), 145.

4. Ibid.

5. John H. Westerhoff III, *Bringing Up Children in the Christian Faith* (San Francisco: Harper and Row, 1980), 52.

6. Rodney Stark, *The Rise of Christianity* (San Francisco: Harper Collins), 88-93.

7. Peter L. Benson and Carolyn H. Eklin, *Effective Christian Education: A National Study of Protestant Congregations—A Summary Report on Faith, Loyalty, and Congregational Life* (Minneapolis: Search Institute, 1990), 66.

8. The parable is told in Howard J. Clinebell Jr., *Basic Types of Pastoral Counseling* (Nashville: Abingdon Press, 1966), 13-14.

9. Kenda Creasy Dean, *Practicing Passion: Youth and the Quest for a Passionate Church* (Grand Rapids, Mich.: William B. Eerdmans Publishing Company, 2004), 26.

10. See Lutheran Volunteer Corps for further ideas on how to organize, prioritize, and envision the program: www.lutheranvolunteercorps.org

Ch. 8: Work and Avocation

1. As quoted in Mitch Albom, *Tuesdays with Morrie* (New York: Doubleday, 1997), 128, 123.
2. Parker J. Palmer, *Let Your Life Speak: Listening for the Voice of Vocation* (San Francisco: Jossey-Bass Publishers, 2000), 8.
3. Juliet Schor, *The Overworked American,* referenced by Dorothy Bass, *Practicing Our Faith,* (San Francisco: Jossey-Bass Publishers, 1997), 75.
4. Sylvia Ann Hewlett, *When the Bough Breaks: The Cost of Neglecting Our Children* (New York: HarperPerennial), 318.
5. Walter Brueggemann, *The Land: Place As Gift, Promise, and Challenge in Biblical Faith,* 2nd ed. (Minneapolis: Fortress Press, 2002), 184.
6. Martin Luther, "The Holy and Blessed Sacrament of Baptism," *Luther's Works,* vol. 44 (Philadelphia: Fortress Press, 1966), 108.
7. Martin Luther, "Holy Sacrament of Baptism" *Luther's Works,* vol. 35 (Philadelphia: Fortress Press, 1960), 41-42
8. Bass, 85.
9. Wayne Muller, *Sabbath: Finding Rest, Renewal, and Delight in Our Busy Lives* (New York: Bantam Books), 3.
10. Ibid., 6.
11. Ibid., 8.
12. Ibid., 10.
13. Parks, 6.
14. Ibid., 182.

Ch. 9: Spiritual Hunger

1. Parks, 16.
2. Ibid.
3. Ibid.
4. Christian Smith and Melinda Lundquist Denton, *Soul Searching: The Religious and Spiritual Lives of American Teenagers* (New York and Oxford: Oxford University Press, 2005), 171.

5. Ibid.
6. Ibid.
7. Martin Luther, *The Magnificat, Luther's Works*, vol. 21, (St. Louis: Concordia Publishing House, 1956), 299.

Ch. 11: Presence, Renewal, and Transformation in Men's Ministry

1. www.risensavior.org/Outreach/Befrienders/index.cfm?Dept=25&subDept=65
2. www.stephenministries.org
3. www.peerministry.org
4. www.youthandfamilyinstitute.org
5. http://buildingchurch.net/g2s.htm or www.churchgrowth.org/cgi-cg/gifts.cgi

About the Authors

David W. Anderson is the Director of Home and Congregational Renewal at the Youth & Family Institute in Bloomington, Minnesota. He is the coauthor of two books, *The Child in Our Hands Leadership Manual,* with Roland D. Martinson, and *Frogs without Legs Can't Hear: Nurturing Disciples in Home and Congregation,* with Paul G. Hill. You can reach David at danderson@theinstitutefrw.org.

Paul G. Hill, noted author and speaker, was the Director of the Center for Youth Ministries of Wartburg Seminary. He will be joining the Children, Youth, and Family Ministry Initiative team at Luther Seminary in St. Paul, Minnesota. You can reach Paul at phill@luthersem.edu.

Roland D. Martinson is Carrie Olson Baalson Professor of Children, Youth, and Family Ministry at Luther Seminary in St. Paul, Minnesota. He is a member of the National Council on Family Relations and author of a number of books, including *Effective Youth Ministry, A Congregational Approach.* You can reach Roland at RMartins@luthersem.edu.

LMM Young Men's Ministry Leadership

Doug Haugen, Director
Doug.Haugen@elca.org
(Work) 773-380-2566
(Cell) 847-971-3086

Nathan Anenson
anensonn@yahoo.com
2481 Como Ave. #176
St. Paul, MN 55108
(Cell) 651-769-3226

Charles Atkins, Jr.
cosmiclogic@comcast.net
Loveoneworld@hotmail.com
507 Grand St. Suite 1-Q
Trenton, NJ 08611
(Cell) 609-284-6018
(Home) 609-396-1500

Sean Forde
sforde21@bellsouth.net
8177 Thames Blvd Unit B
Boca Raton, FL 33433
(Home) 561-479-3472

James (Jim) Greene
fieldsup@hotmail.com
fieldsup@comcast.net
1608 11th Ave. SE
Puyallup, WA 98372
(Home) 253-840-0686
(Cell) 425-802-0771

Mike Haynes
jmhaynes@connections-etc.net
5350 Edinburgh Way
Big Lake, MN 55309
(Home) 763-262-6333
(Cell) 763-370-8615

Eugene Koepke
alge973@hotmail.com
11 E Country Club Dr.
Coram, NY 11727
(Home) 631-732-8254
(Cell) 631-561-3089

Keith Langford
klangford03@yahoo.com
2033 S Truckee St
Aurora, CO 80013
(Home) 303-368-4287
(Cell) 303-358-0494 (best way to reach)

Judson Merrell
jmgtbike@bellsouth.net
jmerrell@ltss.edu
4201 N. Main St. #264
Columbia, SC 29203
(Cell) 704-798-4280

Jason Nordling
jnordling@bwbr.com
Jasnord@comcast.net
1328 130th Ave. NE
Blaine, MN 55434
763-755-3489

Jon Palmquist
jon.palmquist@wartburg.edu
100 Wartburg blvd. #1100
Waverly, IA 50677
(Cell) 303-507-7572

Jedidiah Scharmer
Jscharme@luthersem.edu
2481 Como Ave #225
St. Paul, MN 55108
(Cell) 651-246-1081

Andy Savarin
asavarin@kent.edu
5702 Rhodes Rd Apt E
Kent, Ohio 44240
(Home) 330-677-2364
(Cell) 330-284-3112

Tyler Hauger (LYO REP)
hauger@stolaf.edu
St. Olaf College
1500 St. Olaf Ave.
Northfield, MN 55057-1001
(Cell) 612-720-5511

Other Resources from Augsburg Fortress

The Company You Keep by David Bentall
208 pages, 0-8066-5158-X

Explores the experience of three men who have supported each other in friendship for more than twelve years. He chronicles how friendships can inspire, challenge, and have the potential to transform lives. He provides suggestions for initiating long-term, nurturing friendships. Most importantly, Bentall describes the tremendous benefits such friendships have on all areas of a person's life, including family relationships, physical fitness, self-esteem, and spirituality.

The Spirituality of Men by Philip L. Culbertson
296 pages, 0-8006-3447-0

Sixteen men attempt to lay out what it means to be an adult male Christian. The authors move beyond old stereotypes of manliness and Christian identity to chart new identities, roles, and attitudes. They include men who are deeply in the Christian church and men barely in the church, straight and gay men, white men and African Americans, Protestant and Catholic, younger and older.

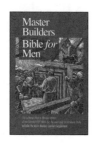

NIV Master Builders Bible for Men
1-5749-4152-6

For small group and personal study, it will assist men in getting to know God, themselves, and each other in a deeper way. With 20,000 study questions written into the text, this Bible provides unlimited opportunities for Bible Study. It also contains six session courses for men, each with a beginner and an advanced track.

Available wherever books are sold.